# Bible Class for Adults and Youth: Beginner's Guide: 2 Kings

**BIBLE CLASS FROM SCRATCH, Volume 12**

Bible Sermons

Published by Guillermo Doris McBride, 2024.

While every precaution has been taken in the preparation of this book, the publisher assumes no responsibility for errors or omissions, or for damages resulting from the use of the information contained herein.

BIBLE CLASS FOR ADULTS AND YOUTH: BEGINNER'S GUIDE: 2 KINGS

**First edition. November 25, 2024.**

Copyright © 2024 Bible Sermons.

Written by Bible Sermons.

# Table of Contents

Introduction ............................................................................. 1

2 Kings 1:1-2:22 ..................................................................... 4

2 Kings 2:23-3:14 .................................................................. 14

2 Kings 3:15-5:7 .................................................................... 23

2 Kings 5:8-6:1 ...................................................................... 33

2 Kings 6:1-25 ....................................................................... 42

2 Kings 6:26-8:10 .................................................................. 52

2 Kings 8:11-9:30 .................................................................. 61

2 Kings 9:31-11:10 ................................................................ 72

2 Kings 11:11-13:2 ................................................................ 81

2 Kings 13:3-15:5 .................................................................. 91

2 Kings 15:8-17:6 ................................................................ 101

2 Kings 17:7-18:16 .............................................................. 111

2 Kings 18:17-19:32 ............................................................ 121

2 Kings 19:33-20:19 ............................................................ 133

2 Kings 20:20-22:6 .............................................................. 142

2 Kings 22:8-23:25 .............................................................. 152

2 Kings 23:26-25:30 ............................................................ 161

Conclusion .......................................................................... 173

**2 Kings 6:6.** *And the man of God said, Where did he fall? And he showed him the place. And he cut down a stick, and cast it there; and the iron swam.*

God can do all things, he can make iron swim-we can't-and yet you see the prophet did it, and he did it by the use of a stick. He cut a stick. Was there any connection between the stick and the iron? I can see none, and yet God uses means, and wants us to use means. "He cut down a stick and cast it there, and the iron swam." If you are in great trouble tonight, have confidence in that God who can make the iron swim. If you have some worry, and you don't know how to deal with it, some job, and you don't know how to do it, look to him who made the iron swim and he can do the same for you. Trust in him, lean on him and see if he does not.

**— Charles Spurgeon**

# Introduction

Originally, the two books formed a single work. One book of Samuel, another of Kings and the third of Chronicles. The division we have today was made by the translators of the Septuagint, the 70 who translated the Old Testament from Hebrew into Greek. Although the author is unknown, we know that this book was written when the First Temple was still standing. Jeremiah has traditionally been considered the author, although modern scholarship assigns literary paternity to a group of writers called "the prophets". The phrase "like David his father" appears 9 times in the First Book of Kings. We follow David's line, and each of the kings was judged by the standard set by David. It was a human standard, but the kings could not even reach that standard. Some parts of this story were unfortunate. As history, they reveal the decline and fall of the kingdom: first the kingdom was divided, and then each of the kingdoms fell.

The moral teaching of these books is to show man his inability to govern himself and the world. In these 4 historical books, we have a very vivid perspective of the rise and fall of the kingdom of Israel. Let us now briefly look at the outline we will follow in our study of these two books of Kings.

First, we have the death of David in chapters one and two of the first book of Kings.

Then we have, secondly, the glory of Solomon's reign, which covers chapters 3 through 11 of 1 Kings. And within that division of the glory of Solomon's reign, we have in chapters 3 and 4 that Solomon asked for wisdom. Chapters 5 to 8 tell us about the construction of the temple.

Chapters 9 and 10 describe the glory of Solomon. And chapter 11 tells of Solomon's difficulties and death.

Thirdly, we have the division of the kingdom, from chapter 12 of 1 Kings to chapter 16 of 2 Kings.

Now, fourthly, we have the captivity of Israel by Assyria, which is found in chapter 17 of the Second Book of Kings. And finally, we have the decadence and captivity of Judah by Babylon, which covers chapters 18 to 25 of the Second Book of Kings.

*Importance of the Second Book of Kings*

Second Kings highlights many unique events and people. Two people were resurrected (2 Kings 4:32-37; 13:20-21). The prophet Elijah left the earth without dying (2 Kings 2:1-18; Enoch was the only other man in the Bible to do so (see Genesis 5:21-24). The waters of the Jordan River receded twice (2 Kings 2:8, 14). These and other miraculous events testified to God's continuing work among His people.

In the period covered by this book, the first written prophets of Israel emerged. Amos and Hosea addressed the people of Israel, while Isaiah, Joel, Micah, Nahum, Habakkuk, Zephaniah and Jeremiah prophesied in Judah; both groups called the people to repentance and warned them of God's coming judgments. The author devotes considerable space to Elisha's ministry after Elijah was taken to heaven, paying special attention to the many miracles Elisha performed.

None of the kings of Israel are described as doing what was right in the eyes of God; each one plunged the people deeper into idolatry. Some of the kings of Judah were righteous, especially Jehoash, Uzziah, Hezekiah and Josiah. Hezekiah defended himself against the Assyrians by fortifying Jerusalem and strengthening his army. Later, Josiah instituted a great spiritual reform. However, none of these efforts were sufficient to prevent God's judgment on the nation during generations of spiritual and moral decay.

*Central idea?*

World affairs played an important role in the fate of Israel and Judah. However, the author of 2 Kings directly links the Israelites' apostasy-led by their wicked kings-to their national destruction and points to it as God's judgment on their stubborn children. Despite repeated warnings from God's prophets to turn from their ways and return to God, the people continued to live in sin. Sadly, they did not believe that God would allow their nation to be destroyed by foreign invaders.

But even after the exile of his people, God did not forget his promise to David. God preserved a remnant of his people and kept the royal line intact so that one day they could return to their land to await the promised deliverer.

*Application*

Second Kings teaches us an important life lesson: Actions have consequences. "Repent!" warned God through the prophets. "Sin will bring judgment". Israel and Judah learned the hard way that God meant business.

*How can we learn? Look at your heart. Is it hard and resistant to God's call? Or can you admit your sin and turn to Him? God is waiting for your answer.*

# 2 Kings 1:1-2:22

Today we begin studying chapter 1 of the Second Book of Kings. In this chapter 1, Moab rebelled against Israel. Ahaziah accidentally fell out of a window and when he wanted to consult Baalzebub, to see if he would be healed of his wounds, he received his judgment from Elijah. Elijah brought fire down from heaven twice, to consume the first two captains sent by Ahaziah, but saved the third captain. God's judgment would be fulfilled with the death of Ahaziah, who would be succeeded by Jehoram on the throne of the kingdom of Israel in the north.

In our last study of the First Book of Kings, we saw that King Ahab had not died on the battlefield due to the good aim of an enemy soldier. Recall that Ahab was disguised as a common soldier so as not to be a favorite target for enemy troops. However, we saw that he died a victim of what we could qualify as an errant arrow, shot without aiming at anyone in particular by a soldier. Now, from a human point of view we would say that Ahab's death was an accident. However, we are sure that in God's records this death was providential. Thus the prophecy of Elijah was fulfilled to the letter, that Ahab would die and that his blood would be licked by dogs, in the same place where Naboth had died. We also saw how Jehoshaphat, who at first perhaps had eliminated the high places of pagan worship, did not destroy them later, when the people restored them. However, he is classified as a good king, because he served God in his own personal life.

1 Kings 22:51 told us that "Ahaziah the son of Ahab began to reign over Israel in Samaria". So we pick up here the story in 2 Kings. In fact, there is no specific division between 1 and 2 Kings. The account of Ahaziah's reign is begun in 1 Kings and concluded in 2 Kings. The king

and the prophet take the place of the priest as God's instruments of communication.

In 2 Kings, in the first chapter, Ahaziah, king of Israel and son of Ahab and Jezebel, fell out of a window in the upper story of his palace and suffered serious injuries. We will begin, then, by reading the first two verses of this chapter 1 of the Second Book of Kings:

> "After Ahab's death, Moab rebelled against Israel. Ahaziah fell out of the window of a room in the house that he had in Samaria and was wounded. Then he sent messengers to them, saying, 'Go and inquire of Baal-zebub, the god of Ekron, whether I will heal these wounds of mine.'"

Now, we believe that he fell because he was drunk. However, this is only conjecture. So, instead of turning to the Lord for help, Ahaziah, greatly influenced by his mother Jezebel, went to consult Baal-zebub the god of Ekron. And the fact that Ahaziah asked for help from an oracle was a direct challenge to the Lord God of Israel. He wanted to know if he would recover from the wounds of that accident. And let's see what verses 3 and 4 tell us:

> "But the angel of the Lord spake unto Elijah the Tishbite, saying, Arise, and go up to meet the messengers of the king of Samaria, and say unto them, Is there no God in Israel, that ye should go to enquire of Baal-zebub the god of Ekron? Therefore thus saith the Lord, Thus saith the Lord, Thou shalt not arise from the bed whereon thou liest, but shalt surely die. And Elijah departed.

This was one of Elijah's last missions. He met the messengers and gave them the following message: "Is there no God in Israel, that ye go to inquire of Baal-zebub the god of Ekron?" And he immediately delivered God's unpleasant prognosis concerning Ahaziah, that he would certainly die. The messengers then, returned and informed the king of what Elijah had said. Let us read verses 7 to 10 of this chapter 1 of the Second Book of Kings, in which we see

## Elijah protected by God

> *"Then the king asked them, 'What was the man like whom you found and who spoke such words to you?' One who had a garment of hair and a leather girdle about his waist, they answered. It is Elijah the Tishbite," the king exclaimed, and immediately sent after him a captain of fifty, with his fifty men. And when he came up to Elijah, he was sitting on the top of the mountain. And the captain said to him, "Man of God, the king has told you to come down. And Elijah said to the captain of fifty, "If I am a man of God, let fire come down from heaven and consume you and your fifty men. And fire came down from heaven and consumed him and his fifty men".*

Recall that Ahaziah, the king, was the son of Jezebel, the woman who had tried to kill Elijah. And it seems that the instructions to kill him were still in effect. And we also see that Elijah was not a man who did not fit in with the social compromises of the court of his time.

Much is said today about the fact that we must learn to communicate and get along with everyone. Now this is not in all cases God's method. The tolerant or conformist attitude of Christians has not made the world listen to the Church. The fact is that the world is not taking her very seriously. Except for electoral reasons, on ethical issues, it overlooks the Church. The world has to listen to Christians proclaiming the Word of God, to make that moral, spiritual reference point reach everyone, backed by a conduct in accordance with the content of the message. Then there will be an effective communication with society.

Elias was able to communicate effectively. They listened to this coarse and vehement character. The captain sent another captain with 50 men and also ordered Elijah to come down from the top of the mountain. But all that came down was fire from heaven that consumed the captain and his men. Verse 13 says:

*"He sent again the third captain of fifty with his fifty men. And that third captain of fifty went up, and kneeled down before Elijah, and besought him, O man of God, I pray thee, let my life and the lives of these thy fifty servants be of some value in thy sight".*

This man implored God's mercy and God granted it. Let us read verses 15 and 16:

*Then the angel of the Lord said to Elijah, "Go down with him; do not be afraid of him. And Elijah arose, and went down with him before the king, and said unto him, Thus saith the Lord, Because thou hast sent messengers to enquire of Baal-zebub the god of Ekron, as though there were no God in Israel whose word to enquire of, thou shalt not arise from the bed whereon thou liest, but shalt surely die".*

Here we see that Elijah boldly repeated the statement confirming God's judgment. And they add verses 17 and 18:

*"And he died according to the word of the Lord which Elijah had spoken. And Jehoram reigned in his stead in the second year of Jehoram the son of Jehoshaphat king of Judah, because Ahaziah had no sons. Now the rest of the acts of Ahaziah, are they not written in the book of the chronicles of the kings of Israel?"*

And thus ended the lineage of the kings Omri and Ahab, in the kingdom of Israel, or the northern kingdom.

## 2 Kings 2:1-22

The main theme here is the transfer of Elijah. This chapter takes us to the end of Elijah's life. We will see that he was translated to heaven in a chariot of fire. Elisha took the place of prominence, being recognized as his successor. The chapter concludes with the serious incident of the bears destroying the irreverent thugs who mocked Elisha.

This chapter 2 relates the rapture of Elijah. Elijah went from Gilgal to Bethel, then to Jericho and then to the Jordan River, accompanied by Elisha, his successor. Elijah promised Elisha a double portion of his spirit if he would witness his departure. Elijah struck the waters of the Jordan with his mantle and they both passed over dryly. He was carried away in a chariot of fire and Elisha saw him ascend into heaven. Elisha then passed over Jordan again, striking the waters with Elijah's mantle. Also the water fountain at Jericho was purified. Now, on his return to Bethel, Elisha encountered a group of thugs who mocked him menacingly.

Let us begin, then, by reading the first 4 verses of this chapter 2 of the Second Book of Kings, which begin the story that will culminate with

## The departure of Elias

*"And it came to pass, when the LORD was about to take up Elijah in a whirlwind to heaven, that Elijah came with Elisha from Gilgal. And Elijah said to Elisha, 'Stay here now, for the Lord has sent me to Bethel. As the Lord lives, and as your soul lives, I will not leave you,' said Elisha to him. So they went down to Bethel. And the sons of the prophets who were at Bethel came out to meet Elisha, and said to him, "Do you know that the Lord is going to take your master away from you today? Yes, I know; but hold your peace," he answered. Elijah said to him again, "Elisha, stay here now, for the Lord has sent me to Jericho. As the Lord lives, and as your soul lives, I will not leave you," Elisha answered him. So they went on to Jericho.*

Here we see that Elijah was trying to get Elisha to stay. But Elisha did not want to leave Elijah, because he knew that Elijah would leave the earth that day. And Elisha wanted to be present when the Lord took him away. Let's continue with verse 5:

*"And the sons of the prophets that were at Jericho came to Elisha, and said unto him, Knowest thou that the Lord will take away thy lord from thee this day? Yes, I know it; but hold your peace, he answered".*

Now, the interesting thing is that today, as in the past, people are turning to all kinds of people and places for information. This is the time when fortune tellers and those who deal in the zodiac and the occult are offering many suggestions for understanding the future and the mysteries of life. The human being is turning to everything and everyone, except God. But, Dear reader, you will not receive any additional information by going to these resources, than what you would receive if you go directly to God. Let us note that the sons of the prophets here had the information that Elijah was going to depart that day. But, Elisha already knew it. That is, they could not tell Elisha anything that he did not already know by revelation from God. Let us now continue reading verses 6 through 8 of this chapter 2 of the Second Book of Kings:

*Then Elijah said to him, "Please stay here, for the Lord has sent me to the Jordan. As the Lord lives, and as your soul lives, I will not leave you," Elisha answered him. And they departed, both of them. But fifty men of the sons of the prophets came and stood in front of them in the distance, while the two of them stood by the Jordan. Then Elijah took his mantle, folded it and struck the waters, and they parted this way and that, and both of them passed through the dry land".*

Recall that the Lord had divided the waters of the Jordan River for Joshua and the people of Israel at least 500 years before this incident.

At this time, the Lord repeated the miracle for Elijah and Elisha. Let us now read verses 9 and 10:

*"As soon as they passed by, Elijah said to Elisha, Ask what you wish me to do for you, before I am taken away from you. And Elisha said, Let me, I pray thee, have a double portion of thy spirit. You have asked a hard thing, Elijah answered him. If you see me when I am taken from you, it will be granted to you; but if not, it will not.*

Now, let us keep this in mind. Elisha, in fact, was a greater prophet than Elijah, as we shall see later on, because of the number and scope of the miracles he performed. He had upon him a double portion of the Spirit of God. Let us now continue with verse 11:

*"And it came to pass, as they were walking and talking, that a chariot of fire, with horses of fire, swept them both away, and Elijah went up to heaven in a whirlwind".*

This was truly a spectacular conclusion to a spectacular life. Let us now move on to verses 12 to 14, where we will see that

## Elisha received a double portion of Elijah's spirit

*"When Elisha saw this, he cried out, 'My father, my father, my father, the chariot of Israel and his horsemen! And he saw it no more.*

Then Elisha took his garments and tore them in two parts. 13Then he took up the mantle that had fallen from Elijah, went back and stood on the bank of the Jordan. 14Then he took up the mantle that had fallen from Elijah, struck the waters, and said, "Where is the Lord, the God of Elijah?

No sooner had he struck the waters in the same way as Elijah, than the waters parted to one side or the other, and Elisha passed over.

Here we see that Elisha then took Elijah's place and demonstrated his faith. He took Elijah's mantle and struck the waters just as Elijah had done before. Now, the power did not reside in Elijah, nor in the mantle, but in God Himself. Elisha knew this very well. But, it is evident that Elisha had the faith that Elijah had, that is, the faith of Elijah's God, and so the waters parted. Elisha had indeed received a double portion of the Spirit of God. Then we see that Elisha asked: Where is the Lord, the God of Elijah? And this, dear reader, is the important question today. Instead of turning to men or women, or methods, or some panacea for help, as so many people do; why don't you turn to the Lord? He is the living God. He is the God and Father of the Lord Jesus Christ. Why don't you go to the Savior?

Elisha took Elijah's mantle, struck the waters and they parted. And he crossed the Jordan River to begin a new phase of his life. Let us now read verses 15 to 16, which detail the times when

## Elisha succeeded Elijah

*"When they saw him, the sons of the prophets who were on the other side at Jericho said, 'The spirit of Elijah rested upon Elisha. And they went at once to meet him, and fell down before him, and said, Here are among thy servants fifty mighty men. Let them go and seek your master now; perhaps the spirit of the Lord has lifted him up and cast him on some mountain or in some valley. Do not send anyone, he said to them".*

The sons of the prophets, who were the students of theology at that time, were still waiting for Elisha on the other bank, and so they saw him divide the waters of the river with Elijah's mantle and cross the Jordan River. They doubted whether Elijah had really been taken away permanently. And they suspected that the Lord had deposited him in some deserted area. What a peculiar idea they had of God! Let us continue reading verses 17 and 18:

*"But they troubled him so much that he was ashamed, and said, Send them away. So they sent the fifty men, and they searched for him three days, but did not find him. When they returned to Elisha, who had remained at Jericho, he said to them, "Did I not tell you not to go?"*

Elijah was indeed gone and that there was no longer any need to look for him. Therefore Elisha said to them, "Did I not tell you not to go?" At last they had to accept the new situation and Elisha's leadership.

Then the men of the city of Jericho approached Elisha with a problem. Let us read verses 19 to 22 of this chapter 2 of the Second Book of Kings:

*"The men of the city said to Elisha, 'Look, the place where this city is placed is good, as my lord sees; but the waters are bad and the land is barren. Bring me a new cruse, and put salt in it, said he. And when they brought it to him, Elisha went to the springs of the waters, and poured the salt in it, and said, Thus saith the LORD, I have healed these waters; there shall be no more death or sickness in them. And the waters are healed to this day, according to the word which Elisha spake.*

Elisha purified the waters. This was his second miracle. Even today it is possible to see these waters in the valley of Jericho. It is said that it is not advisable to drink from these waters because, being out in the open, in this land, they can easily become contaminated. However, some of the people who have visited Israel and have been in this place, have drunk of these waters, and they say that they are still sweet and delicious to the palate. This miracle showed the inhabitants of Jericho that the Lord, and not the false god Baal, the so-called god of fertility, could intervene to annul the aridity and barrenness of their land. And God's permanent action in those springs would be a perpetual reminder of His ability to bring fertility and blessings in the midst of the aridity and barrenness caused by idolatry.

In the physical world, drought already threatens the maintenance of resources indispensable for life. Water is indispensable for survival. Under present conditions, because of the uncertainty that climate change is bringing to many peoples of the earth, and the possibility of great and prolonged droughts, there is serious concern today that this shortage will affect natural and human life in every order, threatening the production of basic foodstuffs. But there is another very important survival, in the spiritual realm, which affects not only life on this earth but also eternal life. And it has to do with alienation from God. That is why in the Old Testament, God sent drought as a punishment because human beings were in a situation of spiritual drought, turning away from God to go back to practicing sin and evil in all its forms. At present, it is necessary to be aware that the material resources produced by man cannot give eternal life to the soul, nor satisfy it in its passage through this world. Human efforts to satisfy it only produce polluted waters, like those waters of Jericho, waters that could not quench thirst. Polluted waters, until God worked the miracle of purifying them. And this incident reminds us that in the New Testament, in the dialogue between Jesus and the Samaritan woman, recorded in the Gospel of John 4, Jesus offered that woman "living water". He said, "Whoever drinks of the water that I will give him will never thirst. For the water that I will give him will gush forth in him like a spring of eternal life". This inner spring cannot be compared to any other water. The Lord was speaking of the Holy Spirit, who brings salvation to the person who believes in Him; and through that person, the spring of that water of life would bring salvation to others. That water, Dear Reader, provides constant satisfaction to the spiritual needs and desires of the one who drinks it. Wouldn't you want to taste it?

# 2 Kings 2:23-3:14

Today we continue studying chapter 2 of the Second Book of Kings. And in the previous chapter, we saw the translation of Elijah and how Elisha took Elijah's place and demonstrated his faith. We also saw that he received a double portion of the Spirit of God. And the sons of the prophets who were still waiting for him on the other side of the Jordan saw how Elisha divided the waters of the Jordan with the mantle of Elijah. And they realized that Elisha had been given some of Elijah's gifts, but they did not understand that Elijah's departure had been permanent. Elisha told them that Elijah had indeed gone and that there was no longer any need to look for him. However, the sons of the prophets insisted to the point that Elisha relented and allowed them to send about 50 men to look for Elijah. But, when they could not find him, they finally had to accept the fact that Elisha was now the prophet of the Lord. Then we saw that the men of the city of Jericho approached Elisha with a problem. It turns out that the waters of their city were not drinkable and the land was barren. Elisha then ordered a new jar filled with salt to be brought to him and then he went out to the springs of the waters and poured the salt in, saying, "Thus says the Lord, I have healed these waters, and there shall be no more death or sickness in them". And the waters were healed unto this day, according to the word of Elisha. And we said that this was the second miracle of Elisha. Now, after all this, there happened an incident that has been criticized more than others that appear in the pages of the Bible and this is recorded in verses 23 to 25 of this chapter 2 of the Second Book of Kings. Before reading them, we will summarize their contents and highlight some background of the situation.

Elisha was returning, after contemplating the transfer of Elijah to heaven, by a chariot of fire. And as Elisha went up to Bethel, the Bible tells us that some boys mocked him. We see that Elisha then cursed them in the name of the Lord and two bears came out of the mountain and killed 42 boys.

Now, not only critics, but also many sincere believers, have stumbled over this portion of Scripture. Those who despise the Bible raise the question of how God would destroy such young men. On the other hand, at first glance, what is recorded here seems to contradict other portions of Scripture.

First of all we need to recognize that when we enter the world, our human minds are more or less neutral. They are neutral on virtually every issue, except the innate trait we all possess, of tending toward rebellion against God. The human being has an instinctive prejudice against God. The natural being is, in the first place, skeptical of everything in the Bible. He will be willing to believe almost anyone, or anything, but God. That reveals the nature of man.

If a person doubts with an honest attitude, he will find that there is an answer to all problems and questions concerning the Word of God.

Elijah had been replaced by Elisha. And Elisha in many respects was greater than Elijah. Now, this statement will no doubt come as a surprise to many, who consider that Elijah was one of the greatest prophets, and possibly one of the witnesses who will one day return to earth during the tribulation, as we see in Revelation chapter 11. Also, if you want to compare these two men according to the miracles they did, you will have to come to the conclusion, that Elisha did more miracles than Elijah did. Elijah was the man to be exposed to the public. Elisha was the one who personally served individuals. His ministry, which unfolded mainly in this area, was not as exciting and dramatic as Elijah's. You will also note that Elisha was a gentle and mild man, in contrast to Elijah.

Elisha, at the beginning of his ministry, was still a young man. Let us note now that at the time of this incident he was returning from beyond the Jordan River, where Elijah had been caught up to heaven in a chariot of fire. News of this event had already spread rapidly throughout that region. By the time Elisha returned from Bethel, there were already many who knew what had happened.

Now, "Bethel" means "house of God". It was first mentioned by Abraham, and then by Jacob. Bethel, however, did not continue to exist in conformity with its name. Let us remember that at the time of the division of the kingdom, Jeroboam placed one of the golden calves at Bethel, so that the people could worship there and thus no longer had to go up to Jerusalem to worship. Also at Bethel there was a school for false prophets. Of course, it was only an imitation of the school of the prophets in Judah. But, it was in this environment that the young men of Bethel were raised. They were ungodly, unbelieving and had no preparation. There was no discipline in their homes. We believe that Bethel was very similar to any of the great cities of today, where there is an almost total indifference or hostility towards God and the knowledge of His will. So, let us remember that Elisha was on his way to Bethel. Let's read this verse 23 of chapter 2 of the Second Book of Kings:

> *"Then Elisha went out from there to Bethel. He was going up the road, when some boys came out of the city and mocked him, saying, 'Come up, you baldheaded man! Come up, you baldheaded man!"*

It is obvious here that some of the boys had left the city. Now, the accepted opinion by many who read this passage is that these were very young, practically children. And if you believe that these boys mentioned here were children, then we will have to admit that Elisha was cruel, because what happened then would be contrary to the teaching of the rest of the Scriptures.

For example, we see that the Lord Jesus said in chapter 19 of the Gospel according to Matthew, verse 14: "Let the little children come to me and do not hinder them, for the kingdom of heaven belongs to such as these. And reading the Bible, one can see God's tender care for the little ones.

Now, let us remember that there at Kadesh-barnea, in Numbers chapter 14, the children of Israel refused to enter the land, giving this excuse, and saying in verse 3: "Why does the Lord bring us into this land to die by the sword, and that our wives and our children should become spoils of war? Would it not be better for us to return to Egypt?" They thought their little ones would be in danger. But, essentially, God said to them, "You should have trusted me. You thought I would not take care of your children. Well, although you will die in the wilderness, your children, whom you thought were in danger, are going to inherit the Promised Land and dwell in it". And in verses 31 and 32 of that same 14th chapter of Numbers, we read that God said to them, "But your children, whom you said would become the spoils of war, I will bring in, and they shall know the land which you despised. As for you, your bodies shall fall in this wilderness".

Frankly, the word naar or nahar in Hebrew, should not be translated as "boys". You will find this same Hebrew word used in other places in the Scriptures, and it does not refer to young boys in the sense of children or toddlers. This word was used of Isaac when he was 28 years old, of Joseph when he was 39 years old, and also for the sodomites who attacked Lot's house. For example, in the First Book of Kings, chapter 12 and verse 8, we read the following, "But he rejected the counsel that the elders had given him, and asked counsel of the young men that were brought up with him, and were in his service". This verse was speaking of the time when Rehoboam forsook the wisdom of the wise elders, and consulted with the young men who had been brought up with him. And the word that is translated there as "young men", is the same word that is translated as "boys" here in chapter 2, verse 23 of this Second Book of Kings. We are sure that no one believes that Rehoboam consulted the affairs of the kingdom with boys or young men of young age. They were young men who had already left childhood and adolescence behind. Let us remember that when Samuel came to anoint one of Jesse's sons as king, his sons were already grown up. As they passed one by one before Samuel, he asked, "Are these all your sons?" Well, well, the word "sons" there, is the same word that we have here in the text that we are studying. And it was used to describe the oldest sons of Jesse. David, Jesse's youngest son wasn't even there. What we have here, then, in this passage from the Second Book of Kings, was a group of young men, not children. They were students in the school of false prophets. They were members of a gang who taunted Elisha by saying to him, "Baldy, come up! baldy, come up!" Now, what did they mean by this? That he should do the same as Elijah had done in ascending to heaven. In other words, they were ridiculing the Biblical truth that God can take people out of this world.

The apostle Peter said that this would be the same attitude that will be revealed again on earth in the last days. And this incident here in chapter 2 of the Second Book of Kings, has been left for us to know that God will judge all those who mock the Second Coming of Christ. The apostle Peter in his second letter, chapter 3, verses 3 and 4 said, "Know ye first of all that in the last days mockers shall come, walking after their own lusts, and saying, Where is the promise of his return? For since the day that the fathers died, all things continue as they were from the beginning of the creation".

So, during the last days on earth there will be those who will mock believers about the second coming of Christ. They will say something like this: "Well, what's the matter, you haven't left yet, are you still around? I thought you were going to leave us. And so, this is the kind of mocking that will be done to believers. And many are already saying: Where is the sign of His coming? Therefore, we should be careful today in how we preach about the second coming of Christ. We should not be isolated or fanatical about the subject. We should treat it with care, which is the way the Word of God treats it. So, the Second Book of Kings is simply a small illustration or figure of the judgment that will come upon those who ridicule or mock the return of Christ to earth. It is a terrible judgment. Now, it says here in verse 24:

*"He looked back and saw them and cursed them in the name of the Lord. Two bears came out of the mountain and tore forty-two of those boys to pieces".*

It is a terrible thing for anyone to deny the deity of Christ and the work He did at His first coming. It is equally tremendous to deny and ridicule the second coming of Christ. He exposes himself to a very severe judgment.

Now, let us observe that these young men called Elisha bald. And this tells us something about this man. We know then that he was not a long-haired man, but that he was bald. The Word of God has much to say concerning judgment. So, Dear reader, we need to understand the facts here. When you understand what is actually taught in this section, you see that there is no teaching here that is foreign to the rest of the Scriptures. Elisha pronounced a curse upon them. And here Elisha sounded like Elijah. He also sounded like the Lord Jesus Christ when he said in chapter 11, verse 21 of the gospel according to Matthew: "Woe to you, O Chorazin, woe to you, O Bethsaida, woe to you, O Bethsaida! For if the miracles had been done in Tyre and Sidon that have been done in you, time that in rough garments and ashes they would have repented". And then he added in verse 23, of the same chapter 11: "And thou, Capernaum, which art lifted up to heaven, into the lowest depths of the pit shalt thou be cast down". That is judgment.

The apostle Paul was able to turn to the soldier who had wounded him and say to him: God will strike you, hypocrite, in Acts chapter 23, verse 3.

And so, Dear Reader, we conclude our study of chapter 2 of the Second Book of Kings.

## 2 Kings 3:1-14

The general theme of chapters 3 and 4 revolves around the miracles of Elisha. The following events are highlighted. The reign of Jehoram, king of Israel, in the north. Moab rebelled against Israel. Jehoshaphat joined with Jehoram to make war on Moab. And once again, Jehoshaphat asked for a prophet from the Lord. Now, at first, Elisha refused, but consented to serve him, because of Jehoshaphat's presence. Elisha announced that God would give them water, something they urgently needed, and predicted then, the victory over Moab, which was given to them.

We will comment on only one or two events that took place in this chapter. Let us read the first 3 verses of this chapter 3 of the Second Book of Kings:

> *"Jehoram son of Ahab began to reign in Samaria over Israel in the eighteenth year of Jehoshaphat king of Judah. He reigned twelve years. But he did evil in the sight of the Lord, though not like his father and mother, for he removed the statues of Baal that his father had made. Nevertheless he gave himself over to the sins of Jeroboam the son of Nebat, who made Israel to sin, and he did not turn from them".*

Joram was the son of Ahab and Jezebel, and successor to his brother Ahaziah, who died childless. He did not sin as Ahab had sinned, but he violated the covenant because it says here that he committed the same sins of Jeroboam, which involved the worship of the golden calf. Let us now read verses 4 and 5:

> "Mesha, king of Moab, owned cattle and paid the king of Israel a hundred thousand lambs and a hundred thousand rams with their wool. But when Ahab died, the king of Moab rebelled against the king of Israel".

Mesha, king of Moab was in a state of servitude to Israel and was obliged to pay tribute to them. When Ahab died, Moab tried to regain his freedom. King Mesha rebelled by refusing to pay tribute. Jehoram therefore gathered his troops and made an alliance with Jehoshaphat, king of Judah, to regain dominion over Moab. At that time, Edom was under the authority of the kingdom of Judah and therefore joined the alliance. Joram suggested that they attack from the south, through the wilderness of Edom, instead of attacking the northern border, which was heavily defended and would have been the more normal way. But since they could not get water for their troops, their campaign was not only halted but they were even in danger of being conquered by the Moabites. Then King Jehoshaphat, who revered God, suggested that they call a prophet of God to lead them. It was a pity that he had not sought such guidance before forming an alliance with Jehoram, the king of Israel. Elisha's response was interesting because it reveals his contempt for Jehoram, king of Israel. Let us read verses 13 and 14:

> But Elisha said to the king of Israel, "What have I to do with you, go to the prophets of your father and to the prophets of your mother? The king of Israel said to him, 'No, for the Lord has gathered these three kings together to deliver them into the hand of the Moabites. Elisha said, "As the LORD of hosts lives, in whose presence I stand, if I did not respect Jehoshaphat king of Judah, I would not look at you or see you.

Elisha's harsh reply to the king of Israel, suggesting that he turn to the prophets of his fathers, implies that since the king was promoting the worship of the pagan god Baal, he should turn to his own god. Elisha was not intimidated by Jehoram's charge, for he knew that God had not led Israel into this distressing situation; the army was at this juncture because of the king's personal initiative. Nevertheless, out of consideration for King Jehoshaphat, the prophet consented to consult the Lord.

Reflecting on the conduct of Jehoram, king of Israel, it is difficult to understand that, despite receiving so much evidence of God's reality and His judgment on his fathers, he would have persisted in living his life with his back turned to God and His Word. By observing him and many other kings and people of all conditions from Biblical times, throughout history and up to our time, it is confirmed that the human being has a natural tendency to move away from God and to oppose Him, and puts it in evidence with behaviors related to his formation and the circumstances that surround him. This situation is a form of slavery, a hopeless bondage, until God sent Jesus Christ into the world. Dear reader, His victory on the cross provides today to everyone who believes in Him, the only possible liberation. Let us remember that when Jesus expounded the mission that had brought Him to this earth in the synagogue at Nazareth, as related by Luke in his Gospel 4:18, He said that He had been sent to bring freedom to the captives. It was as if He had held in His hands the keys to open the door of a great prison. And the impact of His work resembles the irresistible force of that earthquake in the Acts of the Apostles 16 account, which shook the foundations of the Philippian prison, so that all the doors were opened and the chains were loosed. On that memorable occasion, this message of the apostles resounded with clarity: "Believe in the Lord Jesus Christ and you will be saved".

# 2 Kings 3:15-5:7

We continue studying today, chapter 3 of this Second Book of Kings. And in the previous chapter, we saw how Jehoram, Jehoshaphat and Edom, these three kings, were on their way to attack Mesha, king of the Moabites and they had run out of water in the desert. Jehoram then became aware that God had a hand in the disaster they were facing. Jehoshaphat then demanded the presence of a prophet to inform them of God's will. It seems as if Jehoram did not know that Elisha was near. However, to be sure, Elisha was well known for his fame. So much so that one of the servants of the king of Israel knew that he was near. Elisha then came, but had it not been for the presence of King Jehoshaphat, king of Judah, Elisha would not have responded to King Jehoram's request. We will continue today reading verses 15 and 16, of this chapter 3, in a paragraph that we could entitle

## Water and victory

*"But now bring me a musician. While the musician played, the hand of the LORD came upon Elisha, who said, Thus saith the LORD, Make in this valley many pools, For thus saith the LORD, Ye shall not see wind, neither shall ye see rain; but this valley shall be filled with water, and ye shall drink, ye, and your cattle, and your beasts, and your livestock. And because this is a small thing in the sight of the LORD, he will also deliver the Moabites into your hand. And ye shall destroy every fenced city and every fair city, and ye shall cut down every good tree, and ye shall stop all springs of water, and ye shall destroy every goodly land with stones. And it came to pass in the morning, when the sacrifice was offered, that the waters came from Edom, and the land was flooded.*

The ponds would store the water to come. For their part, the Moabite army prepared to defend their country from Israel and, from a distance, they watched their enemy. Let us read verses 22 and 23:

> *"When they arose in the morning and the sun shone on the waters, the Moabites saw from afar the waters red as blood, and said, 'This is blood shed with the sword. The kings have turned one against another, and each has slain his fellow. So to the spoil, Moab!"*

Thinking that the allied kings had fought each other and that the armies had destroyed each other, forgetting all military tactics they set out to collect whatever spoils each could get. This disorder gave Israel an outstanding advantage. Let us continue reading verses 26 and 27:

> *"When the king of Moab saw that he was defeated in battle, he took with him seven hundred men who wielded swords to attack the king of Edom; but they could not do it. Then he took his firstborn, who was to reign in his stead, and sacrificed him as a burnt offering on the wall. This provoked Israel to such great anger that they departed thence and returned to their own land.*

The Moabites widely practiced human sacrifice. No doubt they offered sacrifice to their god Khamosh, hoping that by offering their crown prince, Khamosh would save them from the enemy. Nevertheless, this was for Israel a sign of victory, and a great general impression of the power and mercy of the Lord God of Israel. And thus concludes our study of this chapter 3 of the Second Book of Kings. And we come now to...

## 2 Kings 4

In this chapter 4, we have 5 miracles performed by Elisha. Although there is a similarity between the miracles of Elisha and Elijah, the miracles performed by Elisha were more extensive. First, the widow of one of the prophets was in deplorable circumstances; her two sons were about to be sold into slavery. Elisha then intervened and multiplied her oil. Secondly, a leading woman of Shunem, hosted Elisha and he promised her that she would bear him a son. Thirdly, when the child had grown up, he died and Elisha raised him from the dead, using the same method as Elijah. Fourthly, the sons of the prophets began to eat a poisonous pottage, but Elisha transformed it into a harmless and healthy food. And fifthly, Elisha fed 100 men with the food of one man.

Let us begin, then, by reading the first verse of this chapter 4 of the Second Book of Kings:

*"One of the wives of the sons of the prophets cried to Elisha, saying, 'Your servant, my husband, is dead, and you know that your servant was fearful of the Lord. But the creditor has come to take away two sons of mine as servants".*

The widow of one of the prophets was in deplorable circumstances. Elisha had apparently known her husband. She reminded him that her husband had been a faithful believer. When he died, he left an unpaid debt, which the creditor had come to collect. If the debtor had no personal property as collateral, his own person or those of his dependents would serve as collateral. Consequently, the creditor could legally take the widow's children as payment and make them his slaves. Let us also read verse 2:

*Elisha said to him, "What can I do for you? Tell me what you have in your house. And she answered, Thine handmaid hath not any thing in the house, save a cruse of oil".*

Elisha recognized his responsibility to help this small family. The law of Moses emphasized the care of widows and orphans. Let us continue reading verses 3 to 5:

> *He said to him, "Go and borrow vessels from all your neighbors, empty vessels, as many as you can get. Then go in and shut yourself in with your children. Fill up all the vessels and set aside those that are full. The woman went away and locked herself in with her children. They brought her the jars and she poured out the oil.*

God's provision filled exactly the capacity of the vessels they had and their need. They had there a kind of fountain of oil. And they add verses 6 and 7:

> *When the vessels were full, he said to one of his sons, "Bring me other vessels. There are no more vessels, he answered. Then the oil ceased. She went and told the man of God, who said, Go, sell the oil and pay your creditors; you and your sons live on what is left".*

This was perhaps a greater miracle than the one Elijah had performed in the house of the widow of Zarephath. Let us now read verses 9 and 10, which tell us of another miracle, entitled

## A son for a great woman in Sunem

> *"Then the woman said to her husband, 'Look, I know that this man who always passes by our house is a holy man of God. I pray thee, let us make a little chamber with walls, and put there a bed, and a table, and a chair, and a candlestick, that when he comes to visit us, he may stay in it".*

From time to time Elisha would pass through Shunem and stay in the home of this important woman and her husband. Elisha appreciated the generosity of this home, which was always open to him. And one day, while he was resting, he resolved to reward this thoughtful woman in some way for her kindness, and so he called his servant. Let's see what they talked about in verses 14 to 17:

> *"What then shall we do for her? he said. And Gehazi answered, She has no children, and her husband is old. Call her, said Elisha. And he called*

> her, and she stood in the door. Then Elisha said to her: Next year, by this time, you will hold a son in your arms. And she said, Nay, my lord, thou man of God, do not mock thine handmaid. And it came to pass the next year, that the woman conceived and bore a son, at the time that Elisha had told her".

However, as time went on, the child became ill and died, but

## Life was restored to the Shunammite's son

Elisha restored him using the same method that Elijah had used (1 Kings 17). That is, personal contact with the dead child brought him back to life. The great principle, which relates to other passages of the Bible, is that we were dead in our iniquities and sins, but personal contact with the Lord Jesus Christ brought us to life. In Him we have eternal life, because He is life.

We now move on to another miracle, the one related to

## Poisoned food

The fourth miracle of this chapter (related between verses 38 to 41) refers to the food of the sons of the prophets who were actually students of theology. During a time of famine, one of them went out to gather some vegetables and brought back some fruit. Then they prepared a stew. Let's see what happened by reading verses 40 and 41:

> "Then it was served for the men to eat. But it happened that when they ate of that stew, they began to cry out, "Man of God, there is death in that pot! And they could not eat it. Then Elisha said, "Bring flour. And he sprinkled it into the pot, and said, Give the people something to eat. And there was no longer any evil in the pot".

And so we see how Elisha's miracle consisted in healing the food. Finally, verses 42 to 44 present us with the miracle in which

## One hundred men were fed in a supernatural way

A man, a faithful follower of the Law of Moses, brought the first fruits of the harvest to the sons of the prophets, since Jeroboam had expelled the Levitical priests out of the country. The problem was that that provision was too small to feed 100 men. Let us read verses 43 and 44:

> "His servant answered, How can I serve this to a hundred men? But Elisha insisted, Give the people to eat, for thus saith the Lord, They shall eat, and there shall be enough left over. So the servant served them, and they ate, and there was enough for them, according to the word of the Lord".

This miracle reminds us of the times when the Lord fed multitudes of 4,000 and 5,000 people with a few loaves and fishes. And so we come to the end of this chapter 4 of the second book of Kings. Let us move on to

## 2 Kings 5:1-7

This is one of the most interesting chapters in the life of the prophet Elisha. It reveals that this prophet was probably as tough and determined as Elijah, and he had a good sense of humor. One cannot but smile when reading this episode, even though it is about a man in a very desperate situation. Let us read verse 1, which begins the story of

## The healing of Naaman

> "Naaman, the general of the army of the king of Syria, was a man who enjoyed great prestige in the sight of his lord, who held him in high

*esteem, for through him the Lord had given salvation to Syria. He was a man of great courage, but he was a leper".*

Here we are given a concise sketch of Naaman, general of the Syrian army. Although heathen in his beliefs, he was an important and honorable man. Through him, the Lord had given deliverance to Syria, which was already an extraordinary fact. We can say that the Lord used this man.

Now, you will find that the Lord also uses men who are not Christians. This might seem a little strange, but, one does not have to read much of God's Word to realize that God used men like Pharaoh, Nebuchadnezzar, Cyrus and Alexander the Great. And He used Naaman on this occasion. We are also told that Naaman was a very brave man. All of these things have their value in the Supreme Court of heaven. God does not belittle these characteristics. What was certain was that this pagan was used by God to deliver a people. But, in addition to all these positive facets we have to add the negative one, and that is that he was a leper.

There are many people in the world today about whom many good things can be said, even though they are not Christians. It can be said that great men and women have done good, positive things, even though they are not Christians. But it must also be added that they are sinners. As the apostle Paul says in his letter to the Romans, chapter 3, verse 23: "For all have sinned, and come short of the glory of God". It does not matter how good they are. All, dear reader, are sinners before God.

Now, lepers were not excluded from society in the pagan nations. It is interesting to remember that God gave Israel a law regarding the segregation of lepers, which prevented the spread of the disease. Today, to prevent contagion, it is customary to place lepers in hospitals and colonies, to isolate them from society. God recorded these instructions in His Book centuries before any pagan nation thought it necessary. And this detail must be considered. And it was not until what we would call civilized times that human beings decided to isolate lepers from the rest of society.

Leprosy in the Scriptures is a figure of sin. It was incurable by human means. Only God can cure sin and save a sinner. Naaman, then, a man who had good qualities, was nevertheless a sinner. He tried to cover up his leprosy, but he could not cure it. And so too, many today try in vain to cover up their sins. What they need is to be spiritually cleansed and only Christ can do that. Let's move on now, reading verse 2 of this chapter 5:

> "Armed bands had come out of Syria, and carried away captive out of the land of Israel a damsel, who remained in the service of Naaman's wife".

Now, this was one of those unknown and nameless characters in the Bible. She was a servant, a Hebrew girl, and a great person. To us, she was as great as Queen Esther, as Ruth the Moabitess, as Bathsheba, or as Sarah, Rebecca, and Rachel. It says here that she was in the service of Naamash's wife. And verse 3 says:

> She said to her mistress, "If my lord were to pray to the prophet who is in Samaria, he would heal him of his leprosy".

This Hebrew girl was in no position to give orders, but one fine day she gave a sigh and said, "Would that my Lord would come to see the prophet in Samaria! He would heal him of his leprosy". And this shows that Elisha had a great reputation. Well, someone heard what this girl said and the news reached the king of Syria. And we read in verse 4:

> "Naaman went and told his lord, saying, "This and this has been said by a girl who is from the land of Israel.

The king of Syria was delighted to hear that something could be done for this valuable man and immediately sent him to the king of Israel with a letter of introduction and a valuable gift. Let us continue reading verses 5 to 7:

> *"And the king of Syria answered him, 'All right, go, and I will send a letter to the king of Israel.'"*

So Naaman went out, taking with him thirty thousand pieces of silver, six thousand pieces of gold, and ten changes of garments, 6and he also brought a letter to the king of Israel, saying, "When you receive this letter, you will know by it that I am sending my servant Naaman to you, that you may heal him of his leprosy.

> *"After the king of Israel had read the letter, he rent his clothes and said, 'Am I God, who gives life and takes it away, that this man should send a man to me to heal him of his leprosy? Consider now and see how he seeks occasion against me".*

This letter from the king of Syria asking that the captain of his army be healed of leprosy disturbed and troubled the king of Israel. He then exclaimed, "I am not God. I cannot heal him!" The message had been addressed to the wrong person. The king of Israel did not know what to do with that message, which should have been sent to Elisha. Because Elisha was in contact with the divine Great Physician. So the king of Israel came to the conclusion that the king of Syria was trying to provoke him to quarrel with him. Otherwise, why would he have sent a captain of his army with this impossible request?

And he was absolutely right. Who would be able to erase the indelible marks of leprosy from that man's skin? And, in the same way we ask ourselves today, who will be able to erase from the human soul those stains of sin, wickedness, depravity? These are stains that can be hidden momentarily, they can be made up, but they cannot be erased. In one way or another they surface and become sadly visible. Hence, from remote antiquity comes to us the categorical statement of the patriarch Job in 14:4: "Who shall make clean that which is unclean? No one!" But the reflection between the impossible and the possible, reminds us of an incident in the life of Jesus, recorded in Luke 18, in which some people were reflecting on the difficulties of entering the kingdom of God. Finally, and in a skeptical tone they asked, "Who then can be saved?" Then Jesus answered them, "What is impossible with men is possible with God". Yes, Dear Reader, and if you by faith accept the Lord Jesus Christ as your Savior, you will prove in yourself the truth of that statement in the first letter of the apostle John 1:7: "the blood of Jesus Christ, the Son of God, cleanses us from all sin".

# 2 Kings 5:8-6:1

We continue studying chapter 5 of the Second Book of Kings. And in the previous chapter, we were talking about the young servant of the wife of Naaman, general of the army of the king of Syria. And we said that she was one of those unknown and nameless characters in the Bible. She was a servant, a Hebrew, still young, but a great person. And we said that we considered her as great, perhaps as Queen Esther, or Ruth the Moabitess, or Bathsheba, Sarah, Rebecca or Rachel. As a servant she was in no position to give orders. But one fine day in a subtle way this girl said to Naaman's wife, "Would that my lord would go to the prophet in Samaria! He would heal him of his leprosy". Now, this also shows that Elisha enjoyed great fame. Well, Naaman's wife told Naaman, and Naaman went and told the king. And the king agreed to send Naaman to the land of Israel, giving him some letters for the king of Israel and telling him that he was sending his servant Naaman to heal him.

Now, when the king of Israel read these letters, he said that he was not God. And that he could not heal the man of his leprosy. In other words, the message had been sent to the wrong recipient. The king of Israel thought he saw in this letter that the king of Syria was looking for a pretext to fight against him. What other reason would he have for sending the general of his army with this impossible request? Let us continue today, reading verses 8 through 10 of this chapter 5 of the Second Book of Kings:

*"When Elisha, the man of God, heard that the king of Israel had rent his clothes, he sent to the king, saying, Why hast thou rent thy clothes? Let him come to me, and he shall know that there is a prophet in Israel. So Naaman came with his horses and chariot and stood at the door of*

*Elisha's house. Then Elisha sent a messenger to him, saying, "Go and wash in the Jordan seven times; your flesh will be restored, and you will be clean.*

Naaman was from a great kingdom in the north. The fact is that at that time his nation was defeating the nation of Israel in wars. Syria had already won some victories over Israel, and Naaman expected to be received with great ceremonies. But what happened?

Elisha sent him a message telling him to go and wash seven times in the Jordan River. Now, this hurt Naaman's pride. Elisha actually received this great man in a discourteous manner. The fact is that Elisha did not even receive him. He didn't even come out to the door to greet him. One would have expected the prophet to greet this great general of the Syrian army with a bow. But, instead, Elisha sent his servant to speak to Naaman and tell him what he recommended him to do. Now, would Naaman accept this advice? Well, let's continue reading here verse 11 of this chapter 5:

*"Naaman went away angry, saying, I who thought, "Surely he will go out at once, and standing on his feet he will call on the name of the Lord his God, and lift up his hand, and touch the diseased part, and heal the leprosy".*

Naaman was upset because he was a very proud man. He had never been treated that way before. Now, the Lord was not only going to heal him of his leprosy, but also of his pride. When God saves someone, Dear Reader, He usually removes from his life that which offends. And pride happens to be one of the things that God hates. We hear a lot today about the fact that God is love, but God also hates some things. You cannot truly love without abhorring. You cannot love the good without hating the bad. If you truly love your children, you will hate anyone who causes any harm to your children.

In unequivocal language, God declared that He hates pride in the heart of man. In chapter 6 of the book of Proverbs, verses 16 and 17, it says: "Six things the Lord hates, and seven are an abomination to him: haughty eyes, a lying tongue, hands that shed innocent blood . . etc". And it continues in the following verses, mentioning the other things that God hates. But have you seen what is at the top of God's list? The haughty look. God said he abhors it. He hates haughty eyes, just as much as he hates murder. Now, the apostle James, in the New Testament, in chapter 4 of his letter, verse 6, says, "But he gives greater grace. Therefore he says: God resists the proud, but gives grace to the humble". Pride, Dear reader, is the ruin of human beings, it is a great sin. Once again, in the book of Proverbs, chapter 16, verse 18, we read: "Pride goeth before destruction, and haughtiness of spirit before a fall". And in chapter 11 of the same book of Proverbs, verse 2, it says: "When pride cometh, then cometh shame: but with the humble is wisdom". And finally, in chapter 29 of the same book of Proverbs, verse 23, it says: "The pride of man bringeth humiliation upon him: but the humble in spirit is upheld by honor". Now, why does God abhor pride, pride? One definition of pride says that it is "excessive self-love". It is an inordinate self-love. It is more than a reasonable delight in personal position and achievement. Paul put it this way, in his letter to the Romans, chapter 12, verse 3, saying, "I say therefore, by the grace given to me, to everyone who is among you, not to think of himself more highly of himself than he ought to think, but to think soberly of himself, according to the measure of faith which God has dealt to each one". Pride, then, is to set oneself an excessive price. It is to ask for more than one is really worth.

Have you ever heard the phrase, "I wish I could buy that man for what he is worth, and sell him for what he thinks he is worth?" Well, that is pride. It is the difference between what you are and what you think you are. It was Satan's pride that humbled him. That was his sin. Pride was also the sin of Edom. As for Edom, God said in Obadiah, verse 4:

"Though thou soar as an eagle, and set thy nest among the stars, yet will I bring thee down from thence, saith the Lord".

Human pride is opposed to God's plan, and wherever the two meet, there will always be friction. No compromise is possible. In reality, what happens is a collision, a head-on collision. For God's plan of salvation is the supreme answer to man's pride. God overthrows man. God neither needs nor receives anything from man. When the apostle Paul met the Lord Jesus Christ, he was able to say of himself in his letter to the Philippians, chapter 3, verse 7: "But what things were gain to me, these I counted loss for Christ's sake". In other words, Paul abandoned religion as he understood it, Paul left everything behind, considering it as garbage, renouncing it. Christ and pride, dear reader, cannot be together. You cannot be haughty, proud and at the same time trust in the Lord as our Savior. If you trust in Him, Dear reader, you will have to give up all your pride.

This story of Naaman is the best example we have, of a man who was stripped of his pride. He was a great man, of that there is no doubt. God listed all the qualities that made him stand out as a man of character and ability. But the reality was that he was a leper. He was a sinner. And God not only healed him of his leprosy, but also of his pride. We could go so far as to say that Elisha, with his disdainful attitude, insulted him. As we have already pointed out, Naaman expected another reception from Elisha, that Elisha would go out to meet him, and that he would stand before him calling on the name of the Lord his God, touch him in the place of his leprosy, and he would be healed. And that is what external religiosity is all about. But when God heals a person, he does it through faith. God, in a way, leaves man's pride on the ground. Our healing does not depend on a human being. We must go to God, the Great Divine Physician to be healed. Let us continue, now, reading verse 12 of this chapter 5 of the Second Book of Kings. Naaman continued in anger and said, as we see here in verse 12:

*"Abana and Pharpar, rivers of Damascus, are they not better than all the waters of Israel? If I wash in them, shall I not be clean also? And he was very angry and went away from there".*

In this we agree with Naaman. Those rivers there in Lebanon are beautiful, their waters are clean and emit a soft murmur when they meet the rocks. The Jordan, on the other hand, is a muddy river. Its waters cannot even compare with the beauty of the waters of the rivers of Lebanon. And Naaman said, "Well, why should I go to wash in the Jordan, when there are those rivers which I know so well, with such clean waters?"

Here is some spiritual application for us. There are many who do not like to go to the cross of Christ. It is a place of ignominy, of public affront. It is a place of shame. There are many who do not want to go to the cross. Instead, they prefer to do something important in their own strength. And that is what Naaman wanted to do. Ah, the pride of Naaman! He said that the rivers of Damascus were better, and indeed they were. On the other hand, he was very upset by the insolence and impertinence of the prophet, who commanded him to wash in the Jordan. Returning to our situation, Dear reader, you will have to go to the cross of Christ. No one can go to Christ to present himself before Him as a proud person. When you go to Him, you cannot say that you have something to stand on. You come to Him as you are, in the condition you are in, with no other confidence than that of being received by His love and grace. All you need to do is to accept the work of the Lord Jesus Christ on the cross.

Let us now return to chapter 5 of this Second Book of Kings and read verse 13:

*"But his servants came to him and said, My father, if the prophet commanded you to do a hard thing, would you not do it? How much more, if he has only said to you, Wash, and you shall be clean?"*

Let us observe what Naaman's servants said to him. How many people there are in this world today who would like to do some great work or make some great sacrifice to obtain salvation. But you don't have to do anything. He has already done everything for us. All we need to do is to receive Him. We come to Him as beggars. And let's see, then, what Naaman did, here in verse 14:

> *"Then Naaman went down and dipped himself seven times in the Jordan, according to the word of the man of God, and his flesh became like the flesh of a child, and he was clean".*

Naaman went down to the Jordan and plunged into it seven times according to Elisha's instructions. How we wish we could have been there to see him! We believe that after each dive he looked at himself and perhaps even said, "This is absurd. I'm not getting anything clean. I'm not getting rid of leprosy". And so on and on and on he came out of the water. Until he had come up seven times and found that he had been healed. And we continue reading in verses 15 through 19, to read something about Elisha's servant, specifically

## Gehazi's sin and its punishment

> *"Then he returned with all his companions to where the man of God was, and stood before him, and said to him, 'Now I know that there is no God in all the earth but in Israel. I pray thee, receive, I pray thee, a present from thy servant. But he said, As the Lord lives, in whose presence I stand, I will not accept it. And when he urged him to accept something, Elisha would not. Then Naaman said, I pray thee, shall not thy servant of this land be given the burden of a pair of mules? For from now on your servant shall not sacrifice burnt offerings or offer sacrifices to other gods, but to the Lord. In this may the Lord forgive your servant: when my lord the king goes into the temple of Rimmon to worship there, and leans on my arm, if I also bow down in the temple of Rimmon, if I do such a*

*thing, may the Lord forgive your servant in this. Elisha answered him, Go in peace. So he departed, and walked about half a league of land".*

Now, deeply grateful for his healing, and after recognizing God's reality, Naaman pressed Elisha to accept the valuable gifts he had brought him, as a token of his appreciation and gratitude. But Elisha would not accept any payment for what God had done. On the other hand, he asked special permission from Elisha to accompany the king of Syria in his worship of the idol Rimmon and even to bow down to the idol when his king did so, although he promised not to offer any more sacrifices to other gods, for he would only worship the Lord.

Now, Elisha had a servant named Gehazi. And Gehazi did not like to lose that generous reward. So, he decided to follow Naaman and tell him something to achieve his purpose). Let's see his attitude in verses 21 to 23:

*"Gehazi followed Naaman, and when Naaman saw that he was running after him, he got down from the chariot to meet him, and asked him, 'Is all well? He answered, "All is well. But my lord sent me to say to you, Two young men of the sons of the prophets have just come to me from the mountains of Ephraim; give them, I pray you, three thousand pieces of silver and two new garments. Naaman said, "Please take the two talents. He urged him and tied the two talents of silver in two bags, together with two new garments, and gave it all to two of his servants to carry on their shoulders before Gehazi".*

Let us observe Gehazi's greed and deception to get what he wanted. Let us continue with verses 24 and 25:

*"When he came to a secret place, he took it from their hands and kept it in the house. Then he commanded the men to go away. Then he went in and stood before his master. Elisha said to him, 'Where have you come from, Gehazi? Your servant has not gone anywhere, he answered".*

The servant Gehazi allowed the servants to carry the gifts to a certain place and then put them away himself. He then returned to his work acting as if nothing had happened. But let's see what happened by reading verses 26 and 27:

> *"But Elisha insisted, 'When that man came down from his chariot to meet you, was not my heart also there? Is it time to take silver and to take garments, olive groves, vineyards, sheep, oxen, menservants, and maidservants? Therefore Naaman's leprosy will cling to you and your descendants forever. And he went out from his presence leprous, white as snow".*

Naaman's great sin had been pride. And Gehazi's great sin was greed. Covetousness is the leprosy of the soul. And thus concludes our study of this chapter 5 of the Second Book of Kings. We now turn to

## 2 Kings 6:1

The subject here is the miracle of the floating axe and the danger in Dothan. In this chapter we will see other exciting experiences lived by Elisha. He was an extraordinary prophet, although different from Elijah. Elijah's ministry had been public; but Elisha's was more private. For example, we have seen how he dealt with the problem of Naaman. Elijah had been spectacular; let us remember how he made fire come down from heaven. Elisha, on the other hand, was a quiet person, who rejected public performances. But both were men of God who acted in the time fixed by Him. The first paragraph of this chapter has to do with the miracle of

## The axe

Which we will develop in our next chapter. Our attention is again focused on Elisha. There is no other miracle that reveals so well the character of a person and a prophet as the miracle in which Elisha floated an axe. Let us read verse 1 of this 6th chapter of 2 Kings:

*"The sons of the prophets said to Elisha, "Look, the place where we live with you is narrow for us.*

This episode reveals something of Elisha's popularity. He was a teacher in the school of the prophets, which was like a theological seminary. The school grew and needed larger facilities. This had been due to how well known Elisha was. His testimony as a prophet had made evident the power of God to heal people, to provide food for the needy, water for the thirsty, and to alter the course of events. His faith and dependence on God were an example for these young men who dedicated their lives to developing an effective witness in the midst of their people. In this program we have focused mostly on the healing of Naaman's leprosy. We highlighted the fact that Naaman tried to reward Elisha for being healed. Dear reader, it seems that human beings have not yet grasped the idea that in order to achieve salvation, it is not necessary to reward God, nor is it necessary to try to win his favor through donations, offerings, meritorious works or personal sacrifices. Regarding material goods, St. Peter clearly said in his first letter 1:18; "For you know that you were ransomed from your futile way of life which you inherited from your ancestors not with corruptible things, such as gold or silver, but with the precious blood of Christ". And regarding the value of personal efforts before God, St. Paul was very clear in declaring in his letter to the Ephesians 2:8, "For it is by grace you have been saved through faith; and this is not something you yourselves have obtained, it is the gift of God. Not by works, so that no one can boast of anything".

# 2 Kings 6:1-25

We continue our study of chapter 6 of this Second Book of Kings, which we barely managed to begin in the previous chapter. Actually, we only made an introduction. And we saw that Elisha was an outstanding man. We drew a contrast between him and Elijah. Elijah, for example, was extroverted, but Elisha was introverted. We also mentioned that Elijah's ministry was public and recalled what happened on Mount Carmel, while Elisha's ministry was rather private, as we saw in his way of dealing with Naaman, the general of the Syrian army. Elijah did the spectacular, bringing down fire and rain, but Elisha was an individual of few words. Elijah treated princes. Elisha, on the other hand, dealt with ordinary men. Another difference was that Elijah had not died; on the other hand, Elisha did die. Now, let us read verse 1 of this chapter 6 of 2 Kings, which heads the account of the miracle of

## The axe

*"The sons of the prophets said to Elisha, "Look, the place where we live with you is narrow for us.*

And this episode reveals the popularity of Elisha. Elisha was teaching in a Theological Seminary, that is, in the school of the prophets. Now, the school was growing in number of students and they needed a larger place. And this was undoubtedly due to the presence of Elisha and how well known he was. He was a great teacher. Let's see now what they did and said, with the purpose of enlarging the facilities of the school. Let us now read verse 2 of this chapter 6 of the Second Book of Kings:

> *"Let us go now to the Jordan, and take each of us a beam, and there let us make a place for ourselves to dwell. Go," said Elisha.*

In contrast to the present situation, the students of that time built their own school and when they went out to work, Elisha encouraged them to go. Verse 3 says:

> *"We beg you to come with your servants," said one. I will come, he answered.*

This was a nice personal touch. This detail gives us an idea of Elisha's human character. It reveals how popular he was with the students. Students generally do not want the company of their professors beyond the confines of the campus. But, we already see that here the relationship was different. And we read in verse 4:

> *"So he went with them, and when they came to Jordan, they cut down the wood".*

And then a "little" accident happened that, in other circumstances, would have been qualified as a trivial incident. Verse 5 says:

> *"But it came to pass, as one was felling a tree, that his axe fell into the water, and he cried out, saying, Ah, my lord, it was borrowed!"*

This incident is interesting. It reveals that God is interested in the small events of our lives. When St. Paul wrote to the Philippians, he advised them to pray for everything, that is, nothing was excluded from the sphere of prayer, in the face of which there are no insignificant things.

The loss of the axe might seem insignificant, but for that poor student it was a big problem. In Elisha's time an axe was very important because there was a shortage of any iron tool and even weapons. Of the times of Saul and Jonathan we are told the following, in the First book of Samuel, chapter 13, verse 22: "So it came to pass in the day of battle that none of the people that were with Saul and Jonathan had a sword or spear in his hand, save Saul and Jonathan his son, which had them". In other words, they had 2 swords for a whole army. So we can understand that the loss of an axe was very important for that young man who, of course, had borrowed it.

Now, many Bible commentators have pointed out the carelessness of that student, aggravated by the fact that the tool used was borrowed. The fact was that Elisha, being his teacher, did not address any reproach to him. We believe that Elisha absolved him of all the accusations that had been hurled at him. Evidently there was always the danger of an axe head coming off its handle, and it happened often enough for God to include the possibility of this accident in the law of Moses. The instructions are found in Deuteronomy 19:4 and 5; "4This is the case of the manslayer who may flee there and save his life: he who strikes his neighbor without intent and without having had enmity with him before; 5as he who goes with his neighbor to the mountain to cut wood, and when his hand gives the blow with the axe to cut some wood, the iron of the handle comes loose, and he strikes against his neighbor and he dies. He may flee to one of these cities and save his life". The student involved in this incident revealed to be careful, as he was chopping the wood in the right direction, with no one in front of him, so that when the head of the axe came off, it fell straight into the river. And the axe was borrowed because, given his condition, the man could never have afforded to buy an axe. So we can imagine his displeasure. Let us now read verse 6:

*Where did it fall?" asked the man of God. He showed him the place. Then Elisha cut down a stick, threw it there, and made the axe float".*

Another detail to consider is why Elysium asked him where the axe had fallen. Surely he did this to make it clear that the water was muddy, murky, and the student knew exactly where it had fallen but could not see it so that he could pick it up. If the water had been clear, then he himself could have retrieved it by reaching out his hand. Then some might have argued that Elisha did not really perform a miracle, because the submerged axe would have been easily seen.

This was then a true miracle. It was not spectacular like others, but it was great in its simplicity. We are told that Elisha made the iron float, which was contrary to all known laws of physics. A piece of iron that was at the bottom of the muddy waters of the Jordan River, and that was lifted up, restored to the owner, replaced in the handle, and made useful and functional again constituted a miracle and contains for us today a great spiritual message. The human being resembles the head of an axe. It has slipped off the handle. It has fallen. He is in a state of depravity.

Then Elisha cut a stick and threw it into the waters, which are a symbol of death, of the perdition of the human being, of his distance from God, without being able to enjoy a life with a purpose, of an existence that satisfies him. The stick illustrates the cross on which Jesus Christ died. The Lord descended from heaven to go to that cross, He descended and plunged into the waters of death for you and for me. St. Peter said in his first letter 2:24; "He himself bore our sins in his body on the tree, so that we, being dead to sins, might live a life of righteousness".

Through Christ, Dear Reader, it is possible for man to rise from the waters of death and judgment; he can be placed back in the axe handle, that is, in God's plan and purpose. As the apostle Paul said in his letter to the Philippians, chapter 4, verse 13: "I can do all things through Christ who strengthens me". Human beings no longer need to live an aimless life, a useless life, having an empty and meaningless existence that has driven many people to suicide, because they thought life was not worth living. Dear reader, of course it is not worth living if one finds oneself like that axe head, submerged in the water and in the mud of a river. It is not until Christ lifts us up through His cross by dying for us, and places us within His plans and purposes, that life becomes meaningful and worth living in all its fullness. Recently, a young man said to me, "My life is meaningless, a real failure," and I replied, "Your life has not yet begun and you are telling me that you have failed!" The greatest miracle, Dear Reader, is not to go to heaven in a chariot of fire, like the prophet Elijah, but to go to heaven, to the very presence of God while being sinners, for having trusted in the Lord Jesus Christ. This then is the greatest of miracles; to be rescued from the mire and filth of the world and to receive a new life full of meaning, lived for God, and eternal life. And verse 7 says:

*"Pick it up," said Elisha. The other reached out his hand and picked it up".*

And continuing with the spiritual application, all you have to do is to extend the hand of faith, trust in Him, and appropriate that life, because Jesus Christ died for you, and rose again in order to raise you up and rescue you from that condition. Continuing now, with this chapter 6 of the Second Book of Kings we come to a paragraph titled

## Danger in Dothan

The first sentence reads like a newspaper headline, announcing a war between two countries. It is a conflict that began in biblical times and has continued throughout history. Let's look at the situation, reading verses 8 to 11:

*"Now the king of Syria was at war with Israel, and in counsel with his servants he said, In such and such a place shall my camp be. Then the man of God sent to the king of Israel, saying, 'Do not pass through such and such a place, for the Syrians are going that way. So the king of Israel sent people to the place which the man of God had told him. So he did again and again in order to take care of himself. The heart of the king of*

> *Syria was troubled at this, so he called his servants and said to them, "Will you not discover to me which of us is on the side of the king of Israel?"*

The king of Syria was worried because every plan he prepared and every place he went was discovered by the king of Israel. And he came to the conclusion that there was a spy in his camp. So he gathered his military and tried to discover the traitor. And he did not find him because all his men were loyal to him. Verse 12 says:

> *"One of the servants answered, No, my king and lord; it is Elisha the prophet, who is in Israel, who makes known to the king of Israel the words which thou speakest in thy most secret chamber".*

Here we see that the prophet Elisha had even spied on the bedroom of the king of Syria and knew everything the king of Syria said. Of course, he knew because the Lord had revealed it to him. So the king of Syria decided to eliminate Elisha. The first thing he did was to send spies to find out where he was and they located him in Dothan, about 22 km from Samaria, the capital of the kingdom. Dothan means "two wells" and it was a place with abundant pasture, and where they took the cattle. There was at that time the center of operations of Elisha. Then the king of Syria sent his soldiers who completely surrounded the place. In the morning, Elisha's servant went out, possibly to draw water from one of these wells, and looking about him he saw the city of Dothan surrounded by the Syrian army and was alarmed. He immediately returned and reported to Elisha, asking him a distressing question. "What shall we do? The city is surrounded". Says verse 16:

> *"Elisha answered, 'Do not be afraid, for more are those who are with us than those who are with them.'"*

This answer did not seem realistic, because the armies of Syria were outside, and on the other hand, Elisha and his servant were all alone, and his servant in fear. So Elijah prayed to God, and his prayer was interesting. Let's read verse 17:

> *"And Elisha prayed, saying, I pray Thee, O Lord, open his eyes, I pray Thee, that he may see. Then the Lord opened the eyes of the servant, and he saw that the mountain was full of horsemen and chariots of fire all around Elisha".*

Here the question arises: Is this God's usual and indicated behavior in dealing with his own? On the one hand we hear of Christians who have been especially protected by God in situations of danger and on the other hand, who have not experienced such protection and have become victims of persecution: the latter must have thought that God was not protecting them. Let us return to Dothan, where we believe the answer is to be found. Dothan is mentioned in the Bible only twice, and we believe for a specific reason.

Another man had approached the place. He was a young man of about 17 years of age: danger and fate seemed to await him there. Indeed, he was approaching like a helpless and trusting animal into a trap. His brothers had conspired against him and, after having discussed the matter, the wisest of his brothers recommended selling him into slavery. At that time, that was worse than death, it was like living in a real hell. Yet it was happening to that young man, 17 years old, and he happened to be a man of God. So where were the chariots of fire? Well, the fact that they were not visible does not mean that they were not there. They were there. We can see more evidence of God's protection in Joseph's life than in Elisha's life, even though Elisha performed miracles. However, God never appeared to Joseph, never performed a visible miracle for him. So God used that apparent disaster in his life and later, near the end of his life he was able to say to his brothers, as recorded in Genesis 50:20, "You thought to do evil to me, but God turned it to good". In other words, in Joseph's situation when he was in

Dothan, the chariots of fire were there, they were just used in a different way. In our situation today, although a believer may seem vulnerable and unprotected, difficulties can never reach him without first passing through God's permission and the protection that surrounds believers.

Recall in the book of Job, chapter 1, verse 10, that Satan said to God concerning Job, "Hast thou not surrounded him with thy protection, him and his house and all that he hath? The work of his hands hast thou blessed, and therefore, his goods hast thou increased upon the earth". Dear reader, God is with you; God is for you. If you find yourself in a predicament, in a difficulty, God has allowed you to live that situation. We do not know why. But, He allows certain painful experiences to come into your life for a certain purpose. The apostle Paul told us in his letter to the Romans, chapter 8, verse 28: "And we know, moreover, that all things work together for good to them that love God, to them who are the called according to his purpose". So in Elisha's incident at Dothan, Elisha's servant saw that there was sufficient protection around him. Let us read now, in verse 18, how

## Syrian soldiers were blinded

> *"When the Syrians came down to him, Elisha prayed to the Lord, and said, I pray thee, smite these people with blindness. And the Lord smote them with blindness, according to the request of Elisha".*

Elisha did a rather strange thing here. He asked God to smite the army of the Syrians with blindness, and God did exactly that. Then Elisha led them to Samaria and told them that he was leading them to where he himself was. When they arrived in Samaria, he handed them over to the king of Samaria. The king wanted to kill them, but Elisha said, "Don't kill them... Serve them bread and water; let them eat and drink, and let them return to their masters". Let us now read verse 23 of this chapter 6 of the Second Book of Kings:

*"Then a great meal was prepared for them. When they had eaten and drunk, he sent them away, and they returned to their lord. And there came no more armed bands from Syria into the land of Israel".*

Now, both the power and mercy of the God of Israel, represented by Elisha, must have impacted the king of Syria, who abandoned his war against Israel. However, at a later date, the king of Syria besieged the city of Samaria, as we will see in the next episode. Let us read verses 24 and 25, which tell us about the occasion in which

## Ben-hadad, king of Syria, besieged Samaria.

*"After this it came to pass that Ben-hadad, king of Syria, gathered all his army together, went up and besieged Samaria. In consequence of that siege, there was a great famine in Samaria; so hard was it, that the head of an ass was sold for eighty pieces of silver, and the fourth part of a quart of doves' dung for five pieces of silver".*

The famine became so severe that, as we see, even the head of an ass, which has very little meat and could only be cooked to be used as a broth, reached exorbitant prices. That was truly an inflationary situation.

In this program we have seen in the first episode, how God heard the prayer of the prophet Elisha in the miracle of the axe that floated, and we have already seen the spiritual application, comparing the iron submerged in the mud of the river with the situation of the human being far from God, and seeing what should be the response of all those whose life resembles that of that lost and useless piece of iron. In the second miracle, we were able to see how God's protection was made visible around his own, how God controls our lives, whether or not we are affected by the difficulties or dangers that surround us. The conclusion is that God hears, he is attentive to the cry of the people. When the Lord Jesus Christ was on earth, neither the sound of footsteps nor the tumult of the crowd drowned out the cry of blind Bartimaeus, when he cried out to the Lord to receive his sight. On another occasion, a frail woman, weakened by her infirmity, and pushing her way through the crowd, came close enough to Jesus to touch Him. And He, though He was oppressed by the crowd, said, "Who touched My garments?" That is, He remains alert to our needs, both material and spiritual. Dear reader, we beg you to always remember that, though invisible, He remains very close to each one of us. We remind you of the words of Psalm 34, verse 6, in which David, expressing the reality of his own experience said, "This poor man cried, and the Lord heard him, and delivered him out of all his troubles".

# 2 Kings 6:26-8:10

We continue our journey through chapter 6 of this Second Book of Kings, which we are studying. And in the previous chapter, we were talking about the siege of Samaria by Benadadad king of Syria, causing food to be scarce and sold at very high prices. Verses 26 to 30 reveal the horrible fact that they went to the extreme of eating their children, due to the desperate lack of food. Verse 31 says:

*"And the king exclaimed, God bring upon me the worst of punishments, if the head of Elisha the son of Shaphat be left upon his shoulders today".*

We do not know why the king held Elisha responsible for the horrors of the siege of the city. He probably thought that Elisha had the power to miraculously provide food and was enraged, and was ready to execute him if he did not.

This episode is continued without any pause in the next chapter. This was another exciting incident in the life of the prophet Elisha. Let us now turn to

## 2 Kings 7

In the previous chapter and the beginning of this one, we see that the king sent someone to execute Elisha. However God warned the prophet and gave him the good news that the famine would end the next day. That night, four lepers living outside the besieged city entered the camp of the Syrian army in desperation and found it abandoned. During the night, the Lord had caused the superstitious Syrians to hear a great din, which they interpreted as that of a large approaching army that had been hired to attack them. They fled in panic, leaving behind all their provisions. The lepers then made known to the hungry people of Samaria that there was an abundance of food in the abandoned camp.

You will remember that in the previous chapter, chapter 6, we saw that there was a serious famine so serious that the head of an ass was sold for a very high price: about 80 silver coins. And there was not much meat on an ass's head. We suppose that they could only boil it and prepare a broth. But at what a price! The severe food shortage in the land was surely evidence of God's judgment on His people.

Now, as we begin our study of this chapter 7, we see that in the midst of that situation, Elisha made an extraordinary prophecy. Let us read the first verse of this chapter 7 of the Second Book of Kings:

*"Then said Elisha, Hear ye the word of the Lord, Thus saith the Lord, Thus saith the Lord, At this time to-morrow, at the entering in of Samaria, may seven quarts of meal be bought for one piece of silver, and also, for one piece of silver, may fifteen quarts of barley be bought".*

That meant that the monetary inflation would end. But how could such a thing happen, when they were suffering a real famine? Where would the food come from and how could it be brought into the city when the Syrian army was camped outside the walls not allowing anyone to go in or out? Apparently the king believed Elisha's bold prophecy because he spared his life on that occasion. However, the one who was his right hand mocked this prediction. Verse 2 says:

*"A prince upon whose arm the king leaned, answered the man of God, and said unto him, If the Lord should now open windows in heaven, would this be so? He said, Thou shalt see it with thine own eyes, but thou shalt not eat thereof".*

This prediction was literally fulfilled the next day. Now the scene changes to a group of desperate men outside the city gates. Let us read verses 3 to 5:

> *There were four leprous men at the entrance of the gate, and they said to one another, "Why do we stand here waiting for death? If we try to enter the city, we shall die in it, because of the famine in the city; and if we stay here, we shall die also. Let us go now therefore, and pass over to the camp of the Syrians: if they give us life, we shall live, and if they give us death, we shall die. So they rose up in the evening to go to the camp of the Syrians, and when they came to the entrance of the camp of the Syrians, there was no one there".*

Since those were lepers, they were excluded from life in society and depended on family or friends to bring them food. At a time when the people of the city were starving, of course, there was nothing left for them. As we have already said, leprosy is a figure of sin. The application for us is that before we came to Christ, we were in an equally desperate situation. We were like lepers, dwelling among the dead, without hope and without God in this world.

The lepers, aware that they had nothing to lose, decided to abandon themselves to the mercy of the enemy, but when they arrived at the camp of the Syrians, they found it deserted. But when they arrived at the camp of the Syrians, they found it deserted. What would have happened to that great army of a hundred thousand soldiers or even more? But, let us continue reading now verses 6 and 7 of this chapter 7 of the Second Book of Kings:

> *"The Lord had caused the camp of the Syrians to hear the rumbling of chariots, the noise of horses, and the noise of a great army, so they said to one another: The king of Israel has taken in hire against us the kings of the Hittites and the kings of the Egyptians to come and attack us. So they arose and fled at nightfall, leaving their tents, their horses, their asses, and the camp as it was. They fled for their lives.*

The sound of an approaching army caused the besiegers of the city to panic. The Syrians did not flee in an orderly manner but hastily and each one tried to save himself. They were scattering in the middle of the night and quickly escaped. Verse 8 says:

> *"When the lepers came to the edge of the camp, they went into one tent, ate and drank, and took from there silver and gold and raiment, and went and hid them. Then they returned, went into another tent, and from there they also took things which they went to hide".*

In those days, armies transported all the food they would need. In this case it was a long campaign, being the siege of a city like Samaria, located on a hill. After the Syrian army fled, the lepers went into the camp and ate their fill. And then they found and hid more gold and silver than they could ever need. Verse 9 also says:

> *"Then they said to one another, 'We are not doing well. Today is a day of good news, and we are silent. If we wait until dawn, our wickedness will overtake us. Come now therefore, let us go in and break the news in the king's house".*

Once the excitement had passed and they had calmed down, they began to think that while they were getting their fill of food, the inhabitants of the city were starving. They decided to tell everyone the good news.

There is a great spiritual lesson here for us. Right now you and I are enjoying the Word of God. Today is a day of good news and we sit and delight in that Word, should we not go out and communicate it to others? What are you doing to share God's Word with those who are spiritually starving? We must, then, take care to get God's Word to needy hearts. God expects each of us to use the talents He has given us to proclaim the good news message of God's Word. We must not be silent in this hour of desperate spiritual need.

After the lepers reported the good news, the Israelites went to the abandoned Syrian camp and found enough food to feed an army of several thousand soldiers, due to the enormous abundance of food there. The vendors of Samaria made great sales and it was possible to buy food cheaply. So Elisha's prophecy was literally fulfilled and the prince who had doubted, the king's assistant, was run over and killed by the people, just as God's prophet had predicted. In this regard, we recommend that you read verses 10 to 20, that is, the rest of the chapter that we have summarized, because it contains a vivid and detailed account of the unbelieving attitude of the king when he heard the good news brought by the lepers and the outcome of this incident with the literal fulfillment of the prophet Elisha's prediction.

And thus concludes this chapter 7 of this Second Book of Kings, and we come to

## 2 Kings 8:1-10

The general theme of chapters 8 and 9 is the judgment of the wicked. As for the total content of chapter 8, of which we will only examine 10 verses today, we will say that Elisha predicted a 7-year famine and advised the Shunammite widow to leave the region during those years. She returned after the 7 years, and asked the king to return her land to her. After learning who she was, the king returned them to her. Also, Elisha went to Damascus and predicted the death of the ailing king Benhadad of Syria and the ascension of Hazael to his throne, who in turn would destroy Israel. Hazael declared himself innocent of such plans, but he would carry them out anyway. Also, in this chapter, Jehoram, son of Jehoshaphat, began to reign in Judah, in the southern kingdom. He followed in the footsteps of the kings of Israel because he had married Ahab's daughter. Edom rebelled against him and also Libnah. Joram died, after reigning 8 years. He was succeeded on the throne of Judah by Ahaziah his son, who joined with Jehoram, son of Ahab and king of Israel, to make war against Hazael, king of Syria. Jehoram was wounded during the war. Let us begin, then, by reading the first 2 verses of this chapter 8 of the Second Book of Kings, in order to consider

## Elisha's prediction of famine

*Elisha spoke to the woman whose son he had restored to life, and said to her, "Arise, go, you and all your household, and live wherever you can, for the Lord has called for a famine, which will come upon the land for seven years. Then the woman arose and did as the man of God had said to her: she and her household went and lived seven years in the land of the Philistines.*

Elisha advised this Shunammite woman to leave the land and go to another place because there would be seven years of famine in the land. She believed this prediction and obeyed Elisha. She took her family to the land of the Philistines and they dwelt there during the entire period of the famine. Now, that period of famine, once again, was a judgment of God upon the kingdom of Israel, or the northern kingdom. Events like this famine period are always warnings from God that have taken place throughout history. They have been like warnings for the human race to stop and reflect on their situation and change their behavior and attitude towards God. But let us continue reading verses 3 through 6, in which we see that

## The property of the Shunammite was returned

*"When the seven years were expired, the woman returned from the land of the Philistines, and went and besought the king for her house and for her land. And the king was talking with Gehazi, the servant of the man of God, and said unto him, Tell me, I pray thee, all the wonders that Elisha hath done. And while Gehazi was telling the king how he had restored a dead man to life, the woman whose son he had restored to life came to make supplication to the king for her house and for her land. Then said Gehazi, My king and my lord, this is the woman and this is*

*her son, whom Elisha brought back to life. The king asked the woman, and she told him. Then the king commanded an officer, 'Bring back to him all the things that were his, and all the fruits of his land, from the day he left the land until now.*

When the famine period ended, the Shunammite woman returned to her first home. Apparently, she found that others were now living on her land. At the same time, according to God's providence, the king was inquiring about some of the lesser known works of the prophet. And Gehazi was telling him about when Elisha had raised the Shunammite's son from the dead. The king was moved to hear about how Elisha had raised the Shunammite's son from the dead. And when she, who arrived while they were talking, was presented by Gehazi to the king, then she asked the ruler to give her land back to her and the king gave her more than she had asked for. The king decided that her property had to be returned, including the fruits produced by the land during the time of the widow's absence.

The following paragraph sets forth the terms under which

## Elisha foretold the treachery of Hazael, king of Syria

Thus we have another incident in the life of Elisha, which was truly extraordinary. Recall that King Ben-hadab of Syria had tried to capture Elisha in order to kill him. But now the king was very old and sick. Let us read verse 7:

*"Then Elisha went to Damascus. Ben-hadad, king of Syria, was sick, and they told him, The man of God is come hither".*

The king believed that Elisha would restore him to health. In view of the fact that his own life might be in Elisha's hands, he dared not cause him any harm. And let us see what he did then, here in verse 8:

> "Then the king said to Hazael, "Take a present in your hand, go and meet the man of God, and inquire of the Lord by him, asking, 'Shall I be healed of this disease?"

Hazael went out to meet Elisha. Now, Hazael was the captain of Benhadad's army. There was a reference to him, in the First Book of Kings, chapter 19, verse 15, where we read, "And the Lord said unto him, Go, return by the same way, toward the wilderness of Damascus. And thou shalt come and anoint Hazael king over Syria". In other words, Hazael had already been anointed king many years before. He was to succeed Benhadad on the throne of Syria. Hazael was simply waiting for Benhadad's death. We can understand very well that when the old king died, it was very difficult for the successor, whether it was a son, or a General or anybody else, to shed many tears at the funeral, because that very funeral was what would bring his successor to power. So, Hazael went out to receive Elisha, but we do not think he went out with much enthusiasm. He had with him a very magnificent gift for Elisha, a gift from the king. And verses 9 and 10 say here:

> "So Hazael took a present in his hand from among the goods of Damascus, loaded on forty camels, and went to meet him. When he came, he stood before him and said, 'Your son Ben-hadad, king of Syria, has sent me to ask you, 'Will I be healed of this disease? Elisha said to him, Go and say to him, "You will surely be healed. Yet the Lord has revealed to me that he will surely die".

Now, let's look at the message Elisha gave Hazael. He told him that the king would be healed, which would have happened if Hazael had not interfered. And then he told him that, in fact, King Ben-hadab would die. Elisha evidently knew that Hazael would kill the king, although he did not tell him. This was, instead, what Hazael did want to hear. We can imagine that at that moment he smiled an evil smile, because it implied that he would become the king.

In this last part of our program today we have seen, once again, the maneuvers of a king, Hazael, who had been anointed, and who waited with great ambition for the moment of the death of King Ben-hadab, to take his place. The examples of such attitudes would be so numerous throughout history as to make impossible the task of enumerating, even if only the best known cases. The struggle for power turns people into ruthless beings, without scruples of any kind. Of course, the methods have changed and, many times, the so-called civil death is provoked. Human perversity remains unchanged. However, as we conclude, we wish to recall what we have already stated about the good news of the Word of God. It is that, Dear Reader, in a world where millions of people are struggling in despair, where people are so disappointed that they distrust the good news or even receive it with skepticism or unbelief, we wish to emphasize that the Gospel is very good news, confirmed by all those who have accepted, by faith, the work that the Lord Jesus Christ did for them on the cross and have received Him as their Savior. And just as those messengers who had satisfied their hunger with the delicacies they had eaten, thus freeing themselves from physical death, all over the world millions of men and women have experienced in their lives the coming of Jesus Christ, the Bread of Life, and have drunk of the Water of Life which the Spirit of God has poured into their souls, saving them from spiritual death. Won't you, dear reader, take that step of faith and see how right the Lord Jesus Christ was when he said to his own in the account of the incident in John 6: "The words that I have spoken to you are spirit and they are life".

# 2 Kings 8:11-9:30

Today we continue studying chapter 8 of the Second Book of Kings. And in the previous chapter, we were talking about Elisha and his prophecy regarding the death of Ben-hadad, the king of Syria. We saw that the king of Syria, Ben-hadad, was a sickly old man. And he believed that Elisha could restore him to health. Now, in view of the fact that his own life might be in the hands of Elisha, Ben-hadad dared not cause him any harm. And then king Ben-hadad sent Hazael, who was the captain of his army, and told him to bring a present and go and meet Elisha and inquire of him whether he would be healed of his disease. Now, we remember that there was a reference to Hazael in chapter 19 of the First Book of Kings, verse 15, where we read: "And the Lord said unto Elijah, Go, return by the same way, toward the wilderness of Damascus: thou shalt come, and anoint Hazael king over Syria". In other words, Hazael had already been anointed king. He was to succeed Ben-hadad on the throne of Syria. Hazael was simply waiting for the death of Ben-hadad. It was very difficult for the successor, whether son, or general, or anyone else, to shed tears for the death of a king, because that very funeral, would be the one that would give them access to the throne that they would occupy as successors of the king who had died. So, Hazael went out to receive Elisha, but we do not believe that he went out with much enthusiasm. Hazael, therefore, took with him a great gift for Elisha, from the king. And when he found Elisha he said to him, "Thy son Ben-hadad, king of Syria, hath sent me to thee, saying, Shall I be healed of this disease?" Now, let us notice the message that Elisha gave Hazael. He told him that the king would be healed, which would have happened if Hazael had not interfered. And then he told him that, in fact, King Ben-hadab would die. Elisha evidently knew that Hazael would kill the king, although he did not tell him. This was, instead, what Hazael did want to hear. We can imagine that at that moment he smiled an evil smile, because it implied that he would become the king.

But notice what Elisha did. Let's read verse 11 of this chapter 8 of the Second Book of Kings:

> *"The man of God looked at him steadfastly and stood thus until he blushed. Then the man of God burst into tears".*

Elisha's piercing eyes focused on him until Hazael felt ashamed. Then Elisha began to weep: Let us read verse 12:

> *"Then Hazael asked him, 'Why does my lord weep?' He answered, 'Because I know the evil that you will do to the children of Israel: you will set fire to their strongholds, you will kill their young men with the sword, you will dash their children in pieces, and you will cut open the wombs of the women who are with child.'"*

Hazael was surprised, thinking that Elisha was weeping for King Ben-hadab, who had tried to take his life. But Elisha was not weeping for that king, but because the prophet loved his people. He loved God and he loved the service that God had allowed him to perform as a prophet. The anguish suffered because of Ben-hadad had been intense enough, but Hazael was to bring even greater anguish to the people. Although Elijah had anointed Hazael as king, and Hazael had declared that he would not act wickedly, Elisha knew the future better. Let us now read verses 13 to 15:

> *Hazael said, "Well, what is your servant, this dog, that he should do such great things? Elisha answered, 'The Lord has revealed to me that you shall be king over Syria. Hazael went and stood before his master, who asked him, What did Elisha say to you? He said, He told me that you will surely be healed. But the next day he took a cloth, dipped it in water, and put it on Benhadad's face, and he died. In his place Hazael reigned".*

This was precisely what Elisha had predicted. To better understand the rest of the chapter you can consult a chronological list of the kings of Israel and Judah. Let us read, then, verses 16 to 18:

> *"In the fifth year of Jehoram the son of Ahab, king of Israel, Jehoram the son of Jehoshaphat, king of Judah, began to reign. Until then Jehoshaphat had been king of Judah. Jehoram was thirty-two years old when he began to reign, and he reigned eight years in Jerusalem. He walked in the way of the kings of Israel, as the house of Ahab had done, for a daughter of Ahab was his wife, so he did evil in the sight of the Lord".*

From this it can be understood why God did not favor marriages between people of different religions. Although Jehoram of Judah was the son of a king who believed in God like Jehoshaphat, he married the daughter of Ahab and Jezebel and under their bad influence, he followed in the footsteps of the kings of Israel. Here we can also see that Israel, as a nation, was in decline. Edom and Libnah rebelled against the Israelites. Then Jehoram died and his son Ahaziah became the new king of Judah. He joined forces with Jehoram, king of Israel, to fight against the Syrians. But Joram was wounded and returned to Jezreel to heal from the wounds he suffered in his fight against the Syrians. Verse 29 of this chapter 8 of the Second Book of Kings says:

> *"King Joram returned to Jezreel to recover from the wounds that the Syrians had inflicted on him at Ramoth, when he was fighting against Hazael king of Syria. As Joram son of Ahab was sick, Ahaziah son of Jehoram, king of Judah, went down to visit him in Jezreel".*

In the next chapter we will see what happened to Joram while he was in Jezreel recovering from his wounds. And thus concludes this chapter 9.

## 2 Kings 9:1-30

It begins with a paragraph that tells us that

## Jehu was anointed as king in Israel

In this chapter, Elisha sent one of the sons of the prophets to Jehu at Ramoth-gilead, to anoint him king of Israel, and to pronounce judgment against the house of Ahab. Then the army proclaimed Jehu king of Israel. Jehu, for his part, killed Jehoram, who had been the king of Israel until then. He also killed Ahaziah king of Judah. Jezebel tried to win Jehu by seduction, but he ordered her to be killed as well. Elijah's prophecy of Jezebel's death was then fulfilled, literally. It was the horrific end of a terrible and wicked woman.

As we begin our study of this chapter 9, of the Second Book of Kings, we must keep in mind that Ahaziah the king of Judah went up to visit Joram in Jezreel because Joram had been wounded in battle, and was recovering there from his wounds. Apparently he was very sick. Let us read, then, the first four verses of this chapter 9 of the Second Book of Kings:

*"Then Elisha the prophet called for one of the sons of the prophets and said to him, 'Gird up your waist, take this flask of oil in your hands, and go to Ramoth-gilead. When you get there, you will see Jehu son of Jehoshaphat son of Nimshi there. Go in, have him rise from among his brothers and take him to another room. Then take the vial of oil, pour it on his head, and say, Thus says the LORD: I have anointed you king over Israel. Then open the door and run away without stopping. So the young prophet went to Ramoth-gilead.*

The young prophet did what Elisha had commanded him to do. Now, let us note here, that Elisha was nothing spectacular in what he did. One would have thought that Elisha would not have sent a young prophet to anoint a king, but would have done it himself. Recall that Samuel had anointed Saul as king and had also personally gone to Jesse's house to anoint David. It was natural to believe that Elisha would want to personally anoint Jehu as king; but, he did not want to do so. Instead, he sent a young prophet to anoint Jehu, and Jehu did so secretly and privately. This was probably the reason he sent a young prophet to do so; no one would suspect the motives of a young prophet.

So Jehu was anointed king. He was one of the bloodiest individuals in Biblical history and yet in many respects he did the will of God. Recall that God had said that all the house of Ahab would perish and that of his family, no male descendants would be left in Israel. Let us now read verses 9 and 10 of this chapter 9 of the Second Book of Kings:

*"I will treat the house of Ahab as the house of Jeroboam the son of Nebat and as the house of Baasha the son of Ahijah. Jezebel will be eaten by the dogs in the field of Jezreel, and there will be none to bury her. And she opened the door and ran away.*

Now, this was a repetition of what Elijah had already said would happen to the house of Ahab and Jezebel. And Jezebel would not escape God's judgment because of her wickedness. Let's move forward with verses 11 through 13:

*When Jehu went out to meet his master's servants, they said to him, "Is everything all right? Why did that madman come to see you? You know that man and what he said, he answered. They said to him, "It is a lie; tell us now. Jehu answered, "This and this he has spoken to me: Thus says the Lord: I have anointed you king over Israel. Then every man hastily took his mantle and laid it under Jehu on a high throne. Then they blew the trumpet and shouted, Jehu is king".*

When it was announced that Jehu had been anointed king, the news caused a great commotion among all. They blew the ram's horn and said, "Jehu is king". Meanwhile, Jehoram was sick in Jezreel, and Ahaziah was there visiting him. Now, what would happen in Jezreel?

Verses 14 to 20 deal with the preparation for the coming event, which took place when.

## Jehu executed Jehoram

Now Joram in Jezreel did not know that God had removed him from his throne and had anointed Jehu king of Israel. While Joram and Ahaziah, king of Judah, were there together, the watchman reported that a company was riding up. Joram sent a messenger to ask them if they came in peace. Instead of answering the question, Jehu told him to ride in the group behind him. A second messenger arrived and received the same answer. And another watchman informed Jehoram what we see in verse 20:

> "The watchman said again, "This one also came to them, but he does not return, and the going of him who comes is like the going of Jehu the son of Nimshi, for he comes impetuously.

So the messengers who were sent to meet Jehu never returned to inform the king because Jehu was coming to exterminate the king. So, Jehoram and Ahaziah went out to meet Jehu. Verse 22 says:

> "When Jehoram saw Jehu, he said, "Are you come in peace, Jehu?" He answered, "What peace can there be with the fornications of Jezebel your mother, and her many sorceries?"

Obviously, no loyal subject would have dared to make such a statement about the queen mother, Joram instinctively realized that Jehu was leading a rebellion. Let us continue reading verses 23 and 24:

> "Then Jehoram turned the reins and fled, and cried out to Ahaziah, 'Treachery, Ahaziah! But Jehu drew his bow and struck Joram in the back; the arrow pierced his heart, and he fell in his chariot. When Jehoram was trying to flee, Jehu shot an arrow through his heart.

The next paragraph tells us about the following event and we will see that

## Jehu executed Ahaziah

Jehu had come to Jezreel to execute Jehoram. As we have already said, Ahaziah, king of Judah, was there visiting Jehoram and we can say that he was in bad company, among those descendants of the royal house of Ahab. Ahaziah was in the wrong place at the wrong time. Verses 27 and 28 say:

> "When Ahaziah king of Judah saw this, he fled by the way of the garden house. But Jehu pursued after him, saying, Smite him also that is in the chariot".

He was wounded at the ascent of Gur by Ibleam. But Ahaziah fled to Megiddo, and died there.

> "His servants carried him in a chariot to Jerusalem, and there they buried him with his fathers in his sepulcher in the city of David".

Thus we see, then, that Jehu's followers pursued and mortally wounded Ahaziah. Let us now turn to verse 30, which relates the next event, namely, when.

## Jehu executed Jezebel

> "Then Jehu went to Jezreel. When Jezebel heard of it, she painted her eyes with antimony, bound up her head, and looked out of a window".

We come to the death of Jezebel, the queen mother, a truly horrific incident, but, we have to recognize that she was a wicked and bloody woman. She was a member of the royal family, and was apparently one of the most beautiful women of her time, and of all history.... She was the daughter of Et-baal, king of the Sidonians. As a young woman, Jezebel could be compared to Helen of Troy, Salome, Cleopatra or Catherine de Medici.

The marriage of Ahab and Jezebel was probably the most resounding social event of the year. The most prominent people from the two neighboring kingdoms were present. It was a respectable and majestic event, and even Elijah could not object to the event. All the people of both kingdoms represented in this marriage celebrated it. But, it must be added here also, that the demons of hell and the devil must have celebrated the feast. But, the angels, for their part, must have wept, as if a black bunting had been placed on the gates of heaven. Instead of the sound of wedding bells, a funeral dirge was sung. That was how heaven saw this marriage. The world saw things differently, as it always sees them. Now, why was the world optimistic and heaven pessimistic? Well, because God, dear reader, looks at the heart of man. The human being has only a limited vision of things.

Jezebel, then, was one of the most remarkable women in history. She was capable, influential, and had a dominant personality. Her influence extended over three kingdoms, and her evil influence extended even beyond the course of her lifetime. Her life of ill fame became an adage. Jezebel injected a veritable stream of poison into history. The Scriptures do not mention her again until the book of Revelation, at the end of the Bible.

Her name is suggestive. It means "unmarried, chaste". And we have here an indirect suggestion of an abnormality and a perversion. She was probably very cold and uninterested in sex. She was feminine, but with a masculine touch. Nevertheless, she was attractive and seductive. She was, therefore, the Cleopatra of her times. Strong men yielded to her seductive charms. None resisted her, not even Ahab. She dominated him, and reigned over the northern kingdom, the kingdom of Israel.

She implanted the worship of Baal. She imported four hundred and fifty prophets of Baal and four hundred prophets of Ashtoreth. She was reckless, violent, rapacious and fierce. She killed the prophets of God, and the people of God had to live in hiding. Also, Jezebel arranged the marriage of her daughter to the house of David. During her long reign as Ahab's consort, her will was supreme and no person dared to oppose her, with the sole exception of the prophet Elijah. His crimes were many. Blood flowed in the midst of that people because of her evil influence. No one was able to resist her. For a time it seemed as if God was hiding and doing nothing to stop her.

Finally Jezebel committed her most horrible and outstanding crime. She plotted the death of Naboth so that Ahab could possess her vineyard. This was an act of the utmost cruelty and despotism, committed in cold blood. It was a cowardly act, and heaven could no longer remain silent. God's patience reached a limit and he sent Elijah to announce his judgment. And the day of reckoning came. First Ahab died, and the dogs licked up his blood just as the prophet had predicted they would. And then it was Jezebel's turn. She would be trampled and the dogs would eat her to the point that her corpse could not be decently buried.

Fourteen years had passed since Ahab's death, and Jezebel did not believe that the Word of God would ever be fulfilled in her personal case and remained unmoved. She defied God. She stayed in Jezreel, perhaps believing that Ahab's death was simply a coincidence. He believed that he could get away with murder with impunity and that nothing would happen to him. But, as you know, Dear Reader, there is a law of God written on a gigantic illuminated sign, in every crossroads of life, for all the world to read. It says: "Be not deceived; God cannot be mocked: for whatsoever a man soweth, that shall he also reap". These were the words of the Apostle Paul in his letter to the Galatians, chapter 6, verse 7. And in the Gospel according to Luke, chapter 6, verse 38, the

Lord Jesus Christ himself said: "For with the same measure with which you measure, it shall be measured to you again".

This is one of the most sordid chapters in the whole story. It is horrible, grim, bloody. It is a succession of the most disgusting and repulsive scenes in the pages of history. Now, Jezebel was the queen mother. She had been living in all her luxury in the palace of Jezreel. The terrible prophecy of that man Elijah had not yet been fulfilled. But suddenly from the north there appeared a chariot approaching rapidly, driven furiously by Jehu. He had just killed two kings: the king of Israel and the king of Judah. Jezebel saw that her own son Jehoram had been brutally killed. What was she to do? Well, we see that she painted shadows around her eyes, adorned her hair and looked out of a window. This proud queen still believed that she could seduce her captor and captivate him by her feminine charms. Now, she had a grandson who had already turned twenty-three. In other words, she was no longer young. She was old, and neither lotions nor make-up powders and creams could turn this withered queen into an attractive woman.

The violence and death of kings of Israel and Judah has been one of the characteristics of this story. And the words of judgment announced by the prophet Isaiah seem an echo of that situation: "You have trusted in violence and wickedness, and on them you have leaned, therefore this sin shall be to you as a crack that threatens ruin, spreading out in a high wall, whose fall comes suddenly, suddenly". Violence expresses itself today in different ways at all levels of society. And the growing verbal and physical aggressiveness, which manifests itself in gender violence in families and in our schools and institutes, and which affects children, young people and people in maturity, is an expression of that innate violence that arises from the human heart. If the human being does not have, in the first place, peace with God, he cannot experience it in relation to his fellow human beings. Only God, by His Spirit, can pour lasting peace into the lives of those who receive the Lord Jesus Christ as their Savior. Dear reader, remember that He who was called "Prince of Peace" said: "Peace I leave with you, my peace I give unto you".

# 2 Kings 9:31-11:10

We continue our journey through chapter 9 of the Second Book of Kings. And in the previous chapter, we said that this is one of the most sordid chapters in Biblical history. It is horrible, including bloody scenes, the most disgusting and repulsive in the pages of history. We said that Jezebel was the queen mother. She had been living in luxury in the palace of Jezreel. Now, the terrible prophecy of that man Elijah, whom she had hated so much, had not yet been fulfilled. But suddenly, from the north, Jehu came and in a few moments, killed two kings: the king of Israel and the king of Judah. Jezebel saw that her own son Jehoram had been brutally killed. And what does she do? We saw that she painted shadows around her eyes, adorned her hair and looked out of the window. This proud queen still believed that she could seduce her captor and captivate him with her feminine charms. Let us bear in mind that this woman already had a son who was 23 years old. In other words, she was no longer a young woman and we said that none of her lotions, creams and powders could restore her withered youth. And let's see what she said, here in verse 31 of this chapter 9 of the Second Book of Kings:

> "And when Jehu was coming in at the gate, she said, "Is all well with Zimri, murderer of his lord?"

Surely he meant "May we meet to talk about this matter?" We continue reading verses 32 and 33:

> "Then he lifted up his face to the window and said, 'Who is with me? who? And two or three eunuchs bowed down to him. And Jehu commanded them: Cast her down. And they threw her down, and some of her blood splashed on the wall and on the horses. And he ran her down.

Jehu remained impassive and insensitive to Jezebel's words. In other words, he had no pity for her. Jezebel had never struck him with fear; and she had never been attractive to him. He said, "Cast her down". And the eunuchs threw her down and her body slammed violently to the ground. This, Dear Reader, and what happened next, was a horrifying and terrible picture, an unprecedented tragedy. Despite the circumstances, a queen mother would normally have been treated with more respect. But, it was not so in the case of Jezebel. And we read in verse 34:

*"Then Jehu went in, and when he had eaten and drunk, he said, Go now to the cursed woman, and bury her; for she is a king's daughter".*

How could Jehu eat after committing such a horrifying act? Frankly, he himself was like a demon in human form. He was a rude soldier with no courtesy and certainly no chivalry. All he had was great ambition. He avoided no opportunity to commit a crime. He was thus a depraved and debased being. And we read in verses 35 to 37:

*"But when they went to bury her, they found nothing of her but the skull, the feet, and the palms of her hands. So they went back to tell him. And he said, 'This is the word which God spoke by his servant Elijah the Tishbite: In the inheritance of Jezreel shall the dogs eat the flesh of Jezebel. The body of Jezebel shall be as dung upon the face of the field in the inheritance of Jezreel, so that no man may say, This is Jezebel".*

When Jehu sent his servants to bury Jezebel, the dogs had already devoured her. But, Dear reader, no laughter was heard in heaven because of this. Nor was there any mourning. Only a voice like that of Revelation 19:2, which says: "For his judgments are true and righteous, for he hath judged the great whore that corrupted the earth with her fornication, and hath avenged the blood of his servants at her hand". The Psalmist said the following, in Psalm 91, verse 8: "Surely with thine eyes shalt thou behold and see the reward of the wicked". The prophecy concerning Jezebel was fulfilled. Her horrible death again illustrates the truth expressed in Galatians 6:7, "Be not deceived: God cannot be mocked: for whatsoever a man soweth, that shall he also reap".

## 2 Kings 10

In this chapter 10, now, we will see that God's judgment would continue to fall upon the house of Ahab. The following events are highlighted: the house of Ahab was exterminated when Jehu ordered the slaughter of his 70 sons. Then Jehu personally killed those who remained. Jehu also killed the brothers of Ahaziah, king of Judah. Jehu pretended to turn to Baal worship in order to get the followers of Baal to gather. When they gathered, Jehu ordered them all to be put to death. Jehu thus eradicated Baalism. But we see that he himself did not turn away from Jeroboam's sins. Nevertheless, God recognized and rewarded his actions. Then we see that Israel began to decline as a kingdom. Finally we have the death of Jehu, and his son Jehoahaz then succeeded him on the throne. Let us begin, then, by reading the first three verses of this chapter 10 of the Second Book of Kings, which head the story of

## The judgment on Ahab's house

*"Ahab had in Samaria seventy sons, so Jehu wrote letters and sent them to Samaria to the chief men of Jezreel, to the elders and to the guardians of Ahab's sons, saying, Immediately these letters come to you, as you have your lord's sons, and also have chariots and horsemen, the fortified city and weapons, choose the best and the most upright of your lord's sons, set him on his father's throne, and fight for your lord's house".*

Jehu granted the privilege to Ahab's sons to fight for the throne of Israel. None of those seventy sons were willing to stand against Jehu. Then the elders of Israel, to preserve their own lives, proved their loyalty to Jehu by killing those seventy sons of Ahab. Verse 11 says:

*"Then Jehu slew all that remained of the house of Ahab in Jezreel, and all his princes, and all his kinsmen, and his priests, until there was none left".*

Let us read verses 12 to 14, in which we see that

## Jehu annihilated the royal princes of Judah

*"Then he arose from there to go to Samaria, and on the way he came to a shearing house of shepherds. And he found there the brethren of Ahaziah king of Judah, and asked them, Who are you? And they answered, We are the brethren of Ahaziah, and have come to salute the king's sons and the queen's sons. And he said, Take them alive. And when they had taken them alive, they slew them at the well of the shearing house. They were forty-two men, and there was not one of them left".*

After putting an end to the house of Ahab, Jehu set out to accede to the throne in Samaria. There he met forty-two brothers of Ahaziah king of Judah. And he put them to death as well. It is interesting to note, however, that one of them was spared, and that he was a descendant of the house of Saul. Let us read verse 15 of this chapter 10 of the Second Book of Kings:

*"And when he departed thence, he met Jehonadab the son of Rechab. When he had saluted him, he said to him, 'Is your heart as right as mine is with yours? Jonadab answered, "It is. Since it is, give me your hand. So Jonadab gave him his hand. Then he made him go up with him into the chariot".*

Jehu, even on his way to Samaria, met Jehonadab son of Rechab. And he asked him a single question: "Are you friend or foe?" Jehonadab was the founder of the very strict sect of the Rechabites, mentioned by the prophet Jeremiah. He was undoubtedly an influential man. He apparently sincerely supported Jehu's policy against the house of Ahab and was willing to lend his support by allowing himself to be seen in Jehu's chariot. Let us now read verses 18 and 19, which head the account in which

## Jehu exterminated the Baal worshippers

*"Then Jehu called all the people together and said to them, 'Ahab served Baal a little, but Jehu will serve him much. So call to me all the prophets of Baal, all his servants, and all his priests, and let not one of them be missing; for I have a great sacrifice to make to Baal, and whoever is missing shall die. This Jehu did with cunning, to exterminate those who honored Baal".*

The next thing Jehu did was to gather all the prophets of Baal, issuing a false declaration that he would offer a great sacrifice to Baal. Jehu had no intention of worshiping Baal. When all the prophets were gathered, he put them to death. His sacrifice to Baal was only a trap into which all the prophets of Baal fell. Let us read verse 29, in relation to the fact that

## Jehu continued in the sins of Jeroboam

*"With all that, Jehu did not depart from the sins wherewith Jeroboam the son of Nebat made Israel to sin, and left standing the golden calves that were in Bethel and Dan".*

Even though Jehu killed the prophets of Baal, he did not bind himself to the prophets of God. In other words, Jehu turned to the worship of the calf that Jeroboam had established. He did not worship Baal, nor the gods of the Sidonians, but became involved in the worship of the calf, which apparently had come from the land of Egypt. That is, Jehu did not turn to the Lord; but because he showed zeal and enthusiasm for the Lord's cause, God gave him an earthly reward. That is, he prolonged the reign of his house for four generations. Let us read verse 30:

*"And the Lord said unto Jehu, Because thou hast done well in doing that which is right in mine eyes, and hast done to the house of Ahab according to all that was in mine heart, thy sons shall sit upon the throne of Israel unto the fourth generation".*

Although Jehu was a brutal man, God used the wrath of that man for the recognition of His name and to execute divine justice on those who had bloodied that land with their crimes and injustices. And we read in verse 32 of this chapter 10 of the Second Book of Kings, that

## Israel attacked by Hazael of Syria

*"In those days the Lord began to cut off the territory of Israel. Hazael defeated them on all the borders".*

What happened here? Well, the kingdom of Israel or the northern kingdom was already about to be led into captivity. From that time on there would be a decline that would ultimately result in disaster. Those Israelites would be taken captive to Assyria. The chapter concludes with the death of Jehu, who had reigned over Israel for twenty-eight years.

## 2 Kings 11:1-10

Chapters 11 and 12 develop the theme of Joash, the boy king of Judah. Although the story of Ahab and Jezebel is not exactly a pleasant section and some might think that we are done with it, it is not. While it is true that Jehu had wiped out the entire line of Ahab's descendants in the northern kingdom of Israel, a daughter of Ahab and Jezebel, Athaliah, had married someone from the line of the king of Judah, from the line of David, and at this point she was the queen mother. As a worthy daughter of her fathers, she went even further in her cruelty with an incredibly terrible act. Before commenting in more detail on this chapter, we will say that it is notable for the following events: when Athaliah saw that her son Ahaziah was killed by Jehu, this diabolical daughter of Jezebel tried to destroy the entire royal line. She destroyed all the princes of royal descent, except Joash, who had been hidden by a sister of Ahaziah. When Joash was 7 years old, he was made known to the governors of the kingdom, who in turn conspired to remove the cruel Athaliah from the throne. She was then killed and Joash became king at the age of 7. Also Jehoiada, the priest, led a movement to return to the worship of the Lord. And the Baalism that had invaded Judah was eradicated. Let us begin then our reading of this chapter 11 of 2 Kings, with verse 1, which sets forth the action in which

## Atalía murdered her grandchildren

*"When Athaliah, the mother of Ahaziah, saw that her son was dead, she arose and destroyed all the royal offspring".*

While King Ahaziah lived, Athaliah had actually acted as queen because she controlled her son. In many ways she was like Jezebel. When Ahaziah died, it was up to a grandson of hers to accede to the throne and Athaliah was unwilling to allow this. She feared she would not be able to control him and then she would lose her position of power. So what did she do? She destroyed everyone she could who was part of David's line of descent. In other words, he tried to exterminate all of David's descendants. This was another attempt by Satan to destroy the line of descent that would lead to the Lord Jesus Christ. This was how Satan tried to erase the line of David so that the Savior would not be born. Over the centuries Satan has tried to wipe out the Jews. In Egypt, the Lord preserved Moses and the Jews were not killed and were allowed to leave Egypt. In the book of Esther, Haman tried to exterminate the Jews but his attempt was foiled. Satan was behind each of these attempts. And at this point in our story, this woman, Athaliah, attempted to exterminate that line of David's descendants.

Although she thought she had annihilated all the descendants, she was mistaken, for here we are told that she missed one. Let us read verses 2 and 3:

> *"But Jehosheba, daughter of king Jehoram, sister of Ahaziah, took Joash the son of Ahaziah and smuggled him out from among the king's sons whom they were killing, and together with his nurse hid him from Athaliah in the bedroom, and so they did not kill him. Six years he was hidden with her in the house of the LORD, while Athaliah reigned over the land".*

She came to the throne after her son was killed and for some years, she was ruling alone, which was the way she wanted to exercise power. But in the meantime, the child Joash continued to grow. Let us continue reading verse 4, which explains to us how

## Joash acceded to the throne of Judah

> *"But in the seventh year Jehoiada sent for the captains of hundreds, the captains and the guard, and brought them with him into the house of the Lord. He made a covenant with them on oath in the house of the Lord, and showed them the king's son".*

When Joash was about seven years old, Jehoiada sent for the chiefs, the captains and the guards, and revealed to them that the late king had a son who was still alive. Now, when they heard that there was a son of David's lineage, well, they were encouraged, joyful and hopeful. We believe that anyway, they had had enough of this woman Athaliah, and they took the opportunity to dethrone her. And we continue reading in verses 5 to 7 of this chapter 11 of the Second Book of Kings:

> *"Then he commanded them, 'This is what you are to do: one third of you shall keep the watch of the king's house on the Sabbath. Another third*

*part shall be at the gate of Shur, and another third part at the gate of the guardhouse; so shall you keep the house, that it be not broken into. But the two sections of you that go out on the watch on the Sabbath shall keep the watch of the house of the Lord, next to the king".*

According to verses 8 to 10, the guards were to form a circle around the king, each with his weapons in his hand. So additional precautions were taken to preserve the life of this child, whose life would have been in irremediable danger if Athaliah had been able to approach him, for without any scruple she would have killed him, even if he had been her grandson. For this woman was as ruthless as Jezebel. So the young prince was well protected until the moment when he would be presented in public.

In this program we have seen how God's purpose was fulfilled in the life of those kingdoms, the northern kingdom, Israel, and the southern kingdom, Judah, kingdoms that had previously formed one nation. We have seen how the predictions of the prophets were fulfilled and God, in the face of disobedience and idolatry, which led to intrigues, betrayals and crimes, executed his justice. But we also saw God giving new opportunities to those who, although they followed him, made mistakes. And this is how God has acted in all times. Today, as yesterday, He looks inside people and forgives, giving a new opportunity to those who recognize their mistakes and are willing to rectify them. And to those who have turned away from Him, He continues to speak, calling and waiting, like the father in the parable of Luke 15, waiting for the return of the son who had left home. Dear reader, God will receive you and everyone who wants to have, for the first time, a relationship with Him. The doors of the heavenly home are open to you thanks to the work of the Lord Jesus Christ on the cross.

# 2 Kings 11:11-13:2

We continue our study of chapter 11 of the Second Book of Kings. And in the previous chapter, we were talking about how Jehoash had come to the throne of Judah. When Joash was about 6 years old, Jehoiada, the priest, sent for the leaders, the captains and the guard of Israel and revealed to them that the king had had a son who was still alive. Now when they realized that there was a son, of the lineage of David they rejoiced and felt hopeful. We believe that they had had enough of this woman Athaliah, for they had realized what a bloodthirsty woman she was. Jehoiada therefore gave the chiefs, the captains and the people of the guard of Israel precise instructions concerning the personal safety of Joash, the new king. And we saw that they were to be around the king, each one having his weapons in his hands. So, extra precautions were taken to protect the life of this child, because his life would be in serious danger if Athaliah realized that he was alive. Athaliah's desire, no doubt, was to kill her own grandson. She was as cruel as Jezebel had been. So, the child was protected until such time as he could be presented to the people. We continue, reading verses 11 and 12 of this chapter 11 of the Second Book of Kings:

> "The guard stood in line, every man with his weapons in his hand, from the right side of the house to the left side of the house, by the altar and the temple, around the king. Then Jehoiada brought out the king's son, put the crown and the Testimony on him, and anointed him king. Then they clapped their hands and shouted, Long live the king!"

That was a great day for the southern kingdom, the kingdom of Judah, the day of crowning a king of the seed of David. Let's read verse 13, which begins the account of

## The death of Atalía

*"When Athaliah heard the noise of the people running, she went into the temple of the Lord, where they were all".*

Of course, Athaliah had not been invited to the king's coronation. Evidently she was in David's palace on Mount Zion, from whose height she could see all that was going on in the Temple area. When she heard the shouting and the noise of the people, she went to the temple to see what was going on. And we read in verse 14:

*"She looked and saw the king standing by the pillar, according to the custom, and the princes and the trumpeters standing by the king, and all the people of the land rejoicing and blowing the trumpets. Then Athaliah, tearing her clothes, cried aloud, "Treason, treason!"*

This, of course, was Athaliah's concept of treason. And we continue reading verses 15 and 16 of this chapter 11 of this Second Book of Kings:

*"But Jehoiada the priest commanded the captains of hundreds who ruled the army, 'Bring her out of the temple precincts, and whoever follows her, kill him with the sword. As the priest had said not to kill her in the temple of the Lord, they made way for her and killed her on the way by which the horsemen enter the king's house".*

Athaliah tried to flee, but she had nowhere to go. There was no way to move her trial to another district where she could receive a fair trial. They killed her while she was trying to flee, and thus avoided an appeal to the Supreme Court. As we proceeded in our study, we came to a paragraph that could be entitled

## A renovation

Now, the removal of Athaliah removed a black cloud from the southern kingdom. There was now a new king, but this child had to have advisors to reign in his place, because he was so young. One of those advisors, who had managed everything regarding Joash's ascension to the throne, was Jehoiada the priest. He was the one who had also directed the execution of Athaliah. Let us now read verse 17:

*"Then Jehoiada made a covenant between the Lord, the king, and the people, who were to be the Lord's people; likewise between the king and the people".*

This was the beginning of a return to God. Jehoiada, the priest, then led a movement back to the worship of the Lord. Baal worship had become widespread in those days. It had even been introduced into Judah. We believe that the people still went to the Temple of the Lord but, at the same time, they worshipped Baal. And the same is true today. Many people who profess to be Christians have a religious behavior on Sundays, and then live totally alien to God for the rest of the week. And then they wonder about the lack of vital energy in Christianity today. And now we read verses 18 to 21 of this chapter 11 of the Second Book of Kings:

*"Then all the people of the land went into the temple of Baal and tore it down. They also utterly broke in pieces its altars and its images, and killed Mattan the priest of Baal before the altars. And the priest set a guard at the house of the Lord, and took the captains of hundreds, and the captains, and the guard, and all the people of the land, and brought the king by the way of the gate of the guard, from the house of the Lord unto the king's house. And Jehoash sat on the throne of kings. All the people of the land rejoiced. And because Athaliah had died by the sword by the king's house, the city was quiet. Joash was seven years old when he began to reign".*

This was the beginning of a great spiritual movement that resulted in a great renewal in the kingdom of Judah. There was a general joy at having a descendant of David on the throne and at having removed the wicked foreign usurper and her temple of Baal from the nation. And so we conclude chapter 11 of this Second Book of Kings, and we turn now to

## 2 Kings 12 - The reign of Joash of Judah

In this chapter we have the reign of Joash, who reigned for 40 years and did what was right in the eyes of the Lord. He reestablished the divine worship and repaired the temple. We also see in this chapter that the Syrians took Gath and Joash had to pay Hazael, king of Syria, so that he would stay away from Jerusalem. And finally, Joash was killed by a conspiracy of his servants. And he was succeeded on the throne, Amaziah his son.

We will see that it was Jehoiada who conducted the affairs of his kingdom. At this juncture we would like to make an evaluation of the kings. There were a total of 19 kings, who reigned over the northern kingdom or Israel. There were a total of 20 kings, who reigned over the southern kingdom of Judah. Among the 19 kings who reigned over Israel, none could be considered a righteous king. In fact, the only thing that can be said about them is that they were all wicked. There was no good king among them all.

In the southern kingdom or Judah, there were twenty kings, and only ten of them could have been considered good. Five of these kings were exceptional and during their reigns five periods of reform and renewal took place. We can say that all reform and blessing was incubated in the nest of spiritual renewal. These brief periods of respite kept the fires burning on the altars, which in other times were almost extinguished. Five times the purifying fire of a renewal movement flared up just as a forest fire does, and spread throughout the nation. Of course, it was not a destructive fire, but one of spiritual construction and instruction. God visited His people with comforting times sent from heaven. There was a return to the Word of God and the worship of God. There was power and prosperity.

Dear reader, when a spiritual renewal takes place, a new joy arises in the Church, as well as a renewed power. There will be a new love. First, however, there must be a return to the Bible. A return to the Word of God has produced all the great movements of spiritual renewal. We personally believe that we can experience a great renewal today. Some years ago Dr. Griffith Thomas said, "I see nowhere in the Scriptures that a renewal of the true Church is contrary to the will of God". And Dr. James Gray said: "We do not recall anything in the apostolic letters that justifies the conclusion that the experiences of the early Church cannot be repeated today. Dear reader, let us do our part to spread the Word of God so that God can bring about a real work of grace in our time. In this chapter 12, then, we see Joash behaving like an adult. Let us read, then, the first verse of this chapter 12 of the Second Book of Kings:

*"In the seventh year of Jehu Jehoash began to reign and reigned forty years in Jerusalem. His mother's name was Zibiah of Beersheba".*

Joash began to reign as a child of seven years and continued until he was forty-seven years old. His mother was Zibiah of Beersheba. Let us remember the frequency with which the names of the mothers are mentioned, because they had a great influence on their children. Verse 2 says:

*"Joash did what was right in the sight of the Lord all the time that Jehoiada the priest led him".*

Joash was undoubtedly instructed in the Word of God. And my dear friend, what we need today are men who are instructed in the Word of God and who know God. We need a renewal that can only come to us through the Word of God. Let's read now, verse 3 of this chapter 12 of the Second Book of Kings:

> *"Yet the high places were not taken away, because the people still sacrificed and burned incense on the high places".*

The renewal did not mean that all had turned to God. Many still sacrificed and burned incense in the high places. Even among the priests there were those who had not really experienced a renewal. Let us now proceed to verses 4 and 5:

> *"Joash said to the priests, "All the consecrated money that it is customary to bring to the house of the Lord, the ransom money of each person, as it is appointed, and all the money that each one of his own free will brings to the house of the Lord, 5let the priests receive it, each one from the hands of his relatives, and with it let them repair the porches of the Temple wherever cracks are found.*

The Temple needed some repairs. The priests had been taking the money intended to repair the cracks in the Temple and had been using it for other things. Let's move on now to verses 6 through 8:

> *"But in the twenty-third year of King Jehoash the priests had not yet repaired the breaches of the Temple. Then king Jehoash called for Jehoiada the high priest and the other priests and said to them, 'Why do you not repair the cracks in the Temple? From now on, therefore, do not take any more money from your relatives, but give it to repair the cracks in the Temple. The priests consented to take no more money from the people, nor to have it in their charge to repair the cracks in the Temple".*

It is the same thing that is happening today. Frankly, we believe that the faithfulness of Christians can be tested by the use or abuse of money.

So what did they do to remedy this situation? Well, they prepared an ark for the money to be safely stored, so that the priests would not touch it. Let us read verse 9:

*"But Jehoiada the high priest took a chest and made a hole in the lid, and put it by the altar, on the right hand side as one enters the temple of the Lord, and the priests who kept the door put there all the money that was brought into the house of the Lord".*

We believe that the use of this ark was a good idea. They called it Joash's ark; the money was counted before witnesses, who also took part in the control of its handling.

Now, although a great movement of renewal had taken place, the nation was beginning a period of decadence. Let us read verses 17 and 18 of this chapter 12 of the Second Book of Kings, which tell us how

## Treasures from the temple were used to bribe Hazael

*"About that time Hazael king of Syria came up and fought against Gath and took it. Then Hazael purposed to go up against Jerusalem, so Joash king of Judah took all the offerings which his ancestors Jehoshaphat, Jehoram, and Ahaziah, kings of Judah, had dedicated, and those which he himself had dedicated, and all the gold that was found in the treasuries of the house of the Lord and in the king's house, and sent it to Hazael king of Syria, who withdrew from Jerusalem".*

In other words, King Joash was trying to buy time by bribing Hazael, king of Syria. Let us read verses 19 and 20:

*"Now the rest of the acts of Joash, and all that he did, are they not written in the book of the chronicles of the kings of Judah? His servants arose, plotted a conspiracy, and slew Joash in the house of Milo, as he was going down to Shiloh".*

We will talk more about renewal when we get to the two Books of Chronicles. Joash died at the age of 47. He was killed by his servants and buried with his fathers in the city of David. Jehoash had been a good king. And we will find that his son Amaziah would also be a good king. Amaziah was the ninth king of Judah. Later, Azariah would follow Amaziah on the throne. We will know him also as Uzziah, who reigned during Isaiah's prophetic ministry. It was a great period of the southern kingdom or Juda; but, during this time we will see that the northern kingdom was taken to Babylon for a long period of captivity.

And thus concludes our study of chapter 12 of the Second Book of Kings. We now turn to

## 2 Kings 13:1-2

The general theme refers to the final acts of the prophet Elisha. In this chapter, Jehoahaz, son of Jehu, reigned over Israel for 17 years and followed the bad example of Jeroboam. In desperation, he turned to the Lord, when the king of Syria oppressed him. The Lord delivered them, but they returned to practice the sins of Jeroboam. We have then, the death of Jehoahaz. And Jehoash, Jehoahaz's son, succeeded his father on the throne of Israel or northern kingdom. Nothing of importance was accomplished during his reign, except the fact that he renewed the war against Judah, where Amaziah reigned. Also in this chapter, Elisha fell ill with a fatal disease. Joash, king of Israel, visited him and the prophet promised him victory over the Syrians. Then Elisha died. The Syrians oppressed Israel, but God was kind and merciful to the Israelites.

Dear reader, this is a painful portion of Scripture, and yet it can be very helpful to our heart. This is a very appropriate section for the rulers of the nations. We are following both kingdoms: Israel and Judah. The ten tribes constituted the northern kingdom or Israel and the southern kingdom was constituted by the tribes of Judah and Benjamin. The line of David, reigned in the south. This was the line that would continue directly into the New Testament, and lead to the birth of the Lord Jesus Christ. Now, the line of David was almost eliminated by Athaliah daughter of Ahab and Jezebel, who had married descendants of David, as we saw in chapter 11 of this Second Book of Kings. Here in chapter 13, we will see that

## Jehoahaz reigned over Israel

Jehoahaz son of Jehu reigned over Israel for seventeen years, and followed the example of Jeroboam his father. There was really nothing sensational or interesting about his reign. Many believe that sin brings excitement to life. There is nothing that is as boring as sin, after a while. Instead, Dear Reader, there is real excitement when God is at work. How much we need God to work today. Let us read, then, the first two verses of this 13th chapter of the Second Book of Kings:

*"In the twenty-third year of Joash son of Ahaziah, king of Judah, Jehoahaz son of Jehu began to reign over Israel in Samaria. He reigned seventeen years, but he did evil in the sight of the Lord, for he continued in the sins of Jeroboam the son of Nebat, who made Israel to sin; and he did not depart from them".*

We have already said that Jeroboam was the standard of evil for the northern kingdom of Israel. He instituted calf worship in Israel. That is, he turned Israel away from the worship of the true God and led them into sin, into idolatry. When Ahab and Jezebel came to the throne, they went much further in their wickedness. They implanted active Baal worship, which in reality was demonolatry or demon worship. And now Jehoahaz, like his father Jehu, did not worship Baal, nor did he plunge into the depths of sin as Ahab and Jezebel did. He did, however, go as far as his ancestor Jeroboam went, which was tragic enough.

In this program we have talked about the decadence of the northern kingdom, that of Israel. We have seen how sin and wickedness was rapidly undermining a people and its institutions, beginning at the highest levels of power. As many other kingdoms in history found, there comes a time when it becomes impossible to shore up what is falling, especially if what is falling is being destroyed by the human nature of its rulers and its people. And this destruction takes place first within the people, so that every enterprise they undertake bears within itself the stamp of its irreversible deterioration. Our program today began by describing how a wicked and influential woman was dethroned and lost power, despite having resorted to the most bloodthirsty means to keep it. The prophet Amos once prophesied to the kingdom of Israel and said, in 9:10 that God's judgment would overtake those who, thinking to escape God's deserved punishment, said, "Evil shall not come near us, nor shall it overtake us. But before the punishment, both in the past, through the centuries and in the present, God offers an opportunity to human beings. Said the apostle Paul writing his first letter to his disciple Timothy, 2:4, that God wants all men to be saved and to come to the knowledge of the truth, for there is one God, and one mediator between God and men, who gave himself as a ransom for all. Dear reader, this is the open door to start a relationship with God, this is the way, this is salvation and eternal life, this is your great opportunity.

# 2 Kings 13:3-15:5

In the previous chapter, we began to study chapter 13 of this Second Book of Kings. And we said that in this chapter we see that Jehoahaz, son of Jehu, reigned over Israel for 17 years and that he continued in the sins of his forefather Jeroboam. Actually, we find nothing sensational or interesting about his reign. We mentioned also that Jeroboam was the standard of evil for the kingdom of Israel or the northern kingdom, established the worship of the calf and turned Israel away from the worship of the true God and led the people into sin. When Ahab and Jezebel came to the throne, they did far more evil than he did. They implemented active Baal worship, which was actually demon worship. Now Jehoahaz was like his father. He did not worship Baal, nor did he indulge in the sins of Ahab and Jezebel, but he practiced the sins of Jeroboam and that of course, was bad enough. Let's continue today, reading verses 3 to 5 of this chapter 13 of the Second Book of Kings, where we have

## The repentance of Jehoahaz

*"Therefore the anger of the Lord was kindled against Israel, and for a long time he delivered them into the hand of Hazael king of Syria, and into the hand of Ben-hadad the son of Hazael. But Jehoahaz prayed before the Lord, and the Lord heard him, for he had seen the affliction of Israel, because the king of Syria afflicted them. (And the Lord gave Israel a savior, who brought them out of the power of the Syrians, and the children of Israel dwelt in their tents, as before".*

It says here that Hazael king of Syria came to fight against Jehoahaz. Jehoahaz knew that he was in danger; so, in his fear, he turned to the Lord. And let us observe how gracious God is. The moment the king prayed to God, He heard and answered his prayer. He delivered the people from the oppression of Syria. Dear reader, we must realize what our God is like and how He responds when we cry out to Him. Let us continue reading verses 6 and 7:

> "Yet they departed not from the sins of the house of Jeroboam, who made Israel to sin; in them they walked, and the image of Asherah also remained in Samaria). Jehoahaz had no people left but fifty horsemen, ten chariots, and ten thousand footmen, for the king of Syria had destroyed them and reduced them to the dust that is trodden under foot".

The goodness of the Lord was seen in the life of Jehoahaz, for he answered his cry. But the king and his people continued in their sins and in the worship of their idols. And the king of Syria destroyed Jehoahaz's defenses to such an extent that it was never again possible for him to defend his kingdom properly. Let us now look at the death of Jehoahaz. Let us read verses 8 and 9 of this chapter 13 of the Second Book of Kings:

> "Now the rest of the acts of Jehoahaz, all that he did, and his deeds, are they not written in the book of the chronicles of the kings of Israel? Jehoahaz slept with his fathers and they buried him in Samaria. In his place reigned Jehoash his son.

Here we have the record of the death of Jehoahaz. Another king then came to the throne. His name was identical to that of the king of Judah that we have just studied in the previous chapter. Let us not be confused, then, in this regard. Let us continue reading verse 10, where we are told about

## Joash reigned over Israel

> "In the thirty-seventh year of Jehoash king of Judah Jehoash the son of Jehoahaz began to reign in Samaria over Israel. He reigned sixteen years".

We enter a section of Scripture that leaves one perplexed, because the names of the kings of both kingdoms are similar, and sometimes identical. This makes it difficult to know who was reigning, where he reigned, and the circumstances of his reign. Let us continue reading verse 11:

> "but he did that which was evil in the sight of the Lord: he departed not from all the sins of Jeroboam the son of Nebat, who made Israel to sin, but walked in them".

Here we have to remember that Jeroboam continued to be the standard of evil for evaluating kings. When a king reached his level of sin, God always judged him. Let us now read verse 14 of this chapter 13 of the Second Book of Kings, which tells us about

## Elisha's death: the fulfillment of his prophecy

> "Now Elisha was sick with the disease that would lead to his death, when Joash king of Israel came down to see him, and weeping before him, he said, My father, my father, my father, chariot of Israel and his horsemen!"

Elisha had been like a mighty army for the kingdom of Israel, the northern kingdom, which had not been the case with Elijah. Elisha had been a great help to the king, who was disheartened when the prophet became ill. And we read in verses 15 to 17:

> Elisha said to him, "Take a bow and arrows. So he took a bow and arrows. And Elisha said to the king of Israel, Put your hand on the bow. And he put his hand on the bow. Then Elisha put his hands on the king's hands and said, "Open the window facing east. And when he had opened it, Elisha said to him, Pull. He did so, and Elisha said, The arrow of salvation from the LORD, and the arrow of salvation against Syria. Thou shalt smite the Syrians in Aphek until thou hast destroyed them.

The king visited Elisha, but Elisha did not accept his commiseration and praise. He was still a prophet of God and was giving the king a message from God. He told him what he must do so that he could win the victory over Syria. King Joash was not noted for his faith. Although he was weeping over the dying prophet, he did not have great faith and did not believe that God would grant him victory over Syria. Let us continue reading verses 18 and 19;

> *"Then he said again, 'Take the arrows. And when the king of Israel had taken them, he commanded him, 'Strike the ground. He struck it three times and stopped. Then the man of God, being angry with him, said to him, If you had struck five or six blows, you would have defeated Syria until there were none left, but now you will defeat Syria only three times".*

Discouragement and his lack of faith caused Joash not to strike the ground any more times.

Many great projects for God are never carried out, because the believer who pushes them forward encounters some opposition and experiences discouragement. And then he interrupts his efforts thinking that he was not acting according to God's will. That was the attitude of King Joash when he struck the earth only three times and was interrupted. Many today demonstrate a weak faith, based on illusions and momentary impulses. Dear reader, God has promised us victory, but it is up to us to continue to struggle and persevere, which will increase our faith and expectation to receive God's victory and blessings. Let us now read verses 20 and 21 of this chapter 13 of the Second Book of Kings, which tells us

## The miracle at Elisha's tomb

> *"Elisha died and they buried him. Now when the year was well advanced, armed bands of Moabites came into the land. It happened that some were burying a man when suddenly they saw an armed band; then*

*they threw the corpse into the tomb of Elisha. But as soon as the dead man touched the bones of Elisha, he revived and stood up".*

Even in death, Elisha was a miracle-working individual. What a great strength he had been in that nation! And we continue reading in verses 22 through 25:

*"So Hazael king of Syria afflicted Israel all the days of Jehoahaz. But the Lord had mercy and compassion on them; he turned to them because of his covenant with Abraham, Isaac, and Jacob, and would not destroy them or drive them out from before his face to this day. Hazael king of Syria died, and Benhadad his son reigned in his stead. Jehoash the son of Jehoahaz returned and rescued from the hand of Benhadad the son of Hazael the cities which he had taken from the hand of Jehoahaz his father in war. Jehoash defeated him three times, and restored the cities to Israel".*

Although God was punishing Israel through Hazael of Syria, he did not allow the oppression to go too far. Let us note that God gave him victory three times, according to the faith he had shown. And thus concludes our study of this 13th chapter of the Second Book of Kings.

## 2 Kings 14

The general theme of chapters 14 through 16 is the trajectory of the good and bad kings of Israel and Judah. In this chapter 13, Amaziah, son of Joash ascended the throne of Judah. And he too did what was right in the sight of God. But he did not live like David. He was defeated by Jehoash king of Israel, who took Jerusalem, breached the wall of Jerusalem 180 meters and took away all the gold and silver that was in the house of the Lord. Then Amaziah was killed in a conspiracy at Lachish. Then Azariah, son of Amaziah, ascended the throne. Now, in Israel, Jeroboam II, reigned 41 years and did evil, according to the sins of his ancestor Jeroboam I. He restored the boundaries of Israel, according to the sins of his ancestor Jeroboam I. He reigned 41 years. He restored the boundaries of Israel, according to the words of Jonah, son of Amitai the prophet. This was a historical reference to Jonah, and confirms the fact that Jonah was a true man and prophet in Israel. Jeroboam II later died and his son, Zechariah, succeeded him on the throne. We come to the reign of Amaziah in Judah. As we have already indicated, Amaziah was a good king. The fact is that he was an exceptionally good king. He reigned for 29 years. Let's read, then, the first verse of this chapter 14 of the Second Book of Kings, which reminds us that

## Amaziah reigned over Judah

*"In the second year of Joash son of Jehoahaz, king of Israel, Amaziah son of Joash, king of Judah, began to reign".*

We reiterate that it is good to consult a chronological table of the kings of Judah and Israel, to clarify any confusion when there are two kings with the same name. We thus come to the reign of Amaziah over Judah. As we have already indicated, he was a good king and reigned for 29 years. Let us now proceed with verse 2 of this chapter 14 of the Second Book of Kings:

*"When he began to reign he was twenty-five years old, and he reigned in Jerusalem twenty-nine years. His mother's name was Joadan of Jerusalem".*

Amaziah's mother's name was Joadan. Now, let us observe that the mothers of these kings received the merit that their sons turned out good and the responsibility if they were bad. Amaziah, for example, was a good king. So his mother must have been an extraordinary woman. Let us now read verse 3:

> "He did what was right in the sight of the Lord, though not like David his father, for he did according to all that Joash his father had done".

Amaziah son of Joash, succeeded Joash on the throne of Judah, and we see here that he did what was right before the Lord. However, he did not reach the level of David. We also see that the civil war between the two kingdoms, Judah and Israel, continued. Let us continue reading verses 19 to 22:

> "They conspired against him in Jerusalem, and he fled to Lachish, but they pursued him to Lachish and killed him there. Then they brought him on horses and buried him in Jerusalem with his fathers in the city of David. Then all the people of Judah took Azariah, who was sixteen years old, and made him king instead of his father Amaziah. He rebuilt Elath, and after the king had slept with his fathers, he restored it to Judah".

King Amaziah fled to the city of Lachish, where there was a fortress that offered him a place of refuge, to avoid being captured by the conspirators. Let us continue reading verses 23 to 25, which inform us that

## Jeroboam II reigned over Israel

> "In the fifteenth year of Amaziah son of Joash, king of Judah, Jeroboam son of Joash began to reign in Samaria over Israel. He reigned forty-one years, but he did evil in the sight of the Lord, for he did not turn away from all the sins of Jeroboam son of Nebat, who made Israel to sin. He restored the borders of Israel from the entrance of Hamath to the sea of the Arabah, according to the word of the Lord, the God of Israel, which he had spoken by his servant Jonah the son of Amitai, the prophet who was of Gath-hepher".

Jeroboam II did evil in the sight of the Lord. However, he restored the boundaries of Israel, according to the words of Jonah. And this, here, is a historical reference to Jonah, who wrote a book of the Old Testament and as we said, confirms the fact that Jonah was a true man and a prophet in Israel. (Recall that Jonah was the prophet who preached in the city of Nineveh, whose inhabitants repented). Finally, Jeroboam II died and Zechariah came to the throne, with which we are coming to the account of the end of this nation, which would be carried into captivity. We now move on to

## 2 Kings 15:1-5 - Azariah reigned over Judah

And in this chapter we have, then, the good reign of Azariah. Jotham succeeded him on the throne of Judah in the south. Then, in the north, came a turbulent period. Zechariah, reigning while sick, was assassinated by Shallum. Shallum, who reigned for a month, was in turn assassinated by Manahem. After the death of Manahem, he was succeeded on the throne, Pekahiah his son, who was then murdered by Pekah. Pekah was in turn murdered by Hoshea. Finally, the account returns to the reign in the south, and we have the good reign of Jotham. Let us begin, then, by reading the first 4 verses of this 15th chapter of the Second Book of Kings:

> *"In the twenty-seventh year of Jeroboam king of Israel, Azariah son of Amaziah, king of Judah, began to reign. He was sixteen years old when he began to reign, and he reigned fifty-two years in Jerusalem. His mother's name was Jecholiah of Jerusalem. He did what was right in the sight of the Lord, according to all that his father Amaziah had done. Yet the high places were not taken away, for the people still sacrificed and burned incense on the high places".*

In many respects, Azariah (or Uzziah) was a good king of Judah. However, he did something he should not have done. According to the account in 2 Chronicles 26:15-21, he went into the temple to burn incense on the altar, which was a function reserved for the priests. For this reason he had to suffer a severe punishment and was wounded with leprosy. Let us read verse 5:

*"But the Lord struck the king with leprosy, and he was a leper until the day of his death. The king dwelt in a separate house, and Jotham his son had charge of the palace and ruled the people".*

Now, the prophet Isaiah was saddened when King Azariah died, because he feared that his successors would again lead the nation into idolatry. And his fears were justified, for that is what happened. We will spend more time on this king Azariah (or Uzziah) when we come to the books of Chronicles and Isaiah. Upon the death of Azariah then, his son Jotham, ascended the throne of Judah.

In today's program the story took us to the last actions of the prophet Elisha before his death. And we said that his faith and the influence of his character had constituted a fundamental support for King Jehoash of Israel. Faith was a constant attitude in the life of this prophet. As we have already seen when reading the account of his life, after Moses, he was the person who performed the greatest number of miracles in the Old Testament. The fact is that faith instills great integrity, great confidence and strength to face the difficulties of life. That is why we end today by highlighting the value of faith. And our human nature, which is weak and controlled by the passions, is distrustful. It is always inclined to doubt, to distrust. We remember that Jesus met a man who brought his son to him, who was dominated by the forces of evil and who said to him, "If you can do anything, have mercy on us and help us". Then Jesus answered him, "If you can believe, all things are possible to him who believes". And immediately that distressed father said to Jesus: "I believe: help me in my unbelief". And it is with that attitude, Dear Reader, that we invite you to approach God to begin a relationship with Him, through His Son Jesus Christ, by His work of redemption on your behalf on the cross and by the power of His resurrection. And if you already enjoy that relationship, so that you can turn to Him as His child that you are, and as you naturally share our weakness in the face of life's struggles, you will surely join us in our plea, which is the same desire that His disciples once expressed to Him when they said to Jesus, "Lord, increase our faith".

# 2 Kings 15:8-17:6

We continue our study of this chapter 15 of the Second Book of Kings. And in the previous chapter we talked about Azariah or Uzziah, king of Judah, and we said that he had been a good king, but he had done something that he should not have done, and for which he was punished. And in the Second Book of Chronicles, chapter 26, we find that reason, that Azariah or Uzziah, entered the temple of the Lord to burn incense on the altar of incense, a function that only belonged to the priest. And for that cause, God smote him with leprosy. Now, Isaiah was saddened when Azariah died, because he feared that the nation would have a king who would lead them back to idolatry, and his fears were well founded. We saw later, that when Azariah died, his son Jotham then ascended the throne of Judah. Today, let us consider the reigns of the other kings of Israel. Let us begin by reading verses 8 through 12 of this chapter 15 of the Second Book of Kings:

*"In the thirty-eighth year of Azariah king of Judah, Zechariah son of Jeroboam reigned six months over Israel. But he did evil in the sight of the Lord, as his fathers had done: he did not turn away from the sins of Jeroboam the son of Nebat, who made Israel to sin. And Shallum the son of Jabesh conspired against him, and smote him in the presence of his people, and slew him, and reigned in his stead. The rest of the acts of Zechariah are written in the book of the chronicles of the kings of Israel. This was the word which the Lord had spoken to Jehu: Your sons, even to the fourth generation, shall sit on the throne of Israel. And it was so".*

Now, Zechariah, the last of Jehu's line was killed by Shallum after he had reigned for only six months. And we continue reading verses 13 to 16:

> *"Shallum the son of Jabesh began to reign in the thirty-ninth year of Uzziah king of Judah. He reigned only one month in Samaria, for Manahem the son of Gadi went up from Tirzah, came to Samaria, and smote Shallum the son of Jabesh there. After killing him, he reigned in his place. The other deeds of Shallum and the conspiracy he hatched are written in the book of the chronicles of the kings of Israel. Then Manahem plundered Typhzah and all who were in it, and also its environs, starting from Tirzah. He plundered it because the gates were not opened to him, and he opened the wombs of all the women who were with child.*

Shallum also did not succeed, he reigned for only one month and was defeated and killed by Manahem. Manahem reigned for ten years and did evil, as did Jeroboam. Let us read verses 17 to 22 of this chapter 15 of the Second Book of Kings:

> *"In the thirty-ninth year of Azariah king of Judah, Manahem son of Gadi reigned in Samaria over Israel. He reigned ten years, but he did evil in the sight of the Lord: all his time he did not depart from the sins of Jeroboam son of Nebat, who made Israel to sin. In his time Pul, king of Assyria, came to attack the land. Manahem gave Pul thirty-three thousand pounds of silver to help him confirm himself in the kingdom. Manahem obtained this money from all the mighty and opulent of Israel; each one had to pay a tax of fifty shekels of silver to give to the king of Assyria. Then the king of Assyria turned back, and did not stop there in the country. Now the rest of the acts of Manahem, and all that he did, are they not written in the book of the chronicles of the kings of Israel? Manahem slept with his fathers, and Pekahiah his son reigned in his stead".*

During Manahem's reign, Pul king of Assyria attacked Israel and Manahem had to pay him thirty-three thousand pounds of silver in order to preserve his kingdom. It was a dark period for the nation.

Manahem did evil just as his ancestor Jeroboam had done. Then, we read in verses 23 to 26:

> *"In the fiftieth year of Azariah king of Judah, Pekahiah the son of Manahem reigned two years in Samaria over Israel. And he did evil in the sight of the Lord: he did not turn away from the sins of Jeroboam the son of Nebat, who made Israel to sin. And Pekah the son of Remaliah, his captain, conspired against him, and smote him in Samaria, in the palace of the king's house, with Argob and Arie, and fifty men of the sons of the Gileadites. After he had killed him, he reigned in his place. The rest of the acts of Pekahiah, and all that he did, are written in the book of the chronicles of the kings of Israel".*

That is, upon the death of Manahem, Pekahiah his son followed him on the throne, but he reigned only two years, when Pekah his captain conspired and murdered him. Now, in verses 27 to 31, we read:

> *"In the fifty-second year of Azariah king of Judah reigned Pekah the son of Remaliah in Samaria over Israel. He reigned twenty years, and did evil in the sight of the Lord: he departed not from the sins of Jeroboam the son of Nebat, who made Israel to sin. In the days of Pekah king of Israel came Tiglath-pileser king of Assyria, and took Ijon, and Abel-beth-maachah, and Janoah, and Kedesh, and Hazor, and Gilead, and Galilee, and all the land of Naphtali, and carried the inhabitants thereof captive into Assyria. And Hoshea the son of Elah conspired against Pekah the son of Remaliah, and smote him to death, and reigned in his stead in the twentieth year of Jotham the son of Uzziah. The rest of the acts of Pekah, and all that he did, are written in the book of the chronicles of the kings of Israel".*

So, during the reign of Pekah, *Tiglath-Pileser* king of Assyria attacked Israel and took captive the tribe of Naphtali. Pekah was then killed by Hosea. We now leave the kingdom of Israel in the north, and turn our attention to the kingdom of Judah in the south, specifically to the son of Azariah or Uzziah. Let us read verses 32 and 33, of this chapter 15 of the Second Book of Kings, where we see that

## Jotham reigned over Judah

> *"In the second year of Pekah son of Remaliah, king of Israel, Jotham son of Uzziah, king of Judah, began to reign. He was twenty-five years old when he began to reign, and he reigned sixteen years in Jerusalem. His mother's name was Jerusha the daughter of Zadok.*

Jotham replaced his father, Azariah or Uzziah, as king of Judah and was rated as a good king and, as in other cases, his mother's name was recorded, although he tolerated idolatry, which would eventually send the people into captivity. In this section, we actually overlook the reign of Uzziah. We will look at it in greater detail when we come to the Books of Chronicles and also the Book of Isaiah. And so, then, we conclude our study of this 15th chapter of the Second Book of Kings.

## 2 Kings 16

In this chapter, Ahaz, son of Jotham acceded to the throne of Judah. He was a bad king, who continued in the bad way of the kings of Israel. Rezin, king of Syria and Pekah, king of Israel, invaded Judah, but it was not possible for them to take Jerusalem. Ahaz, for his part, asked Assyria for help and the Assyrians took Damascus.

As we begin chapter 16, we will say that if you like history, you will find this section especially interesting. And if you are looking for spiritual lessons, you will find some very practical ones in this section. Much of this part of God's Word is extremely helpful. Remember that all these things happened to serve as examples for us. Let us begin, then, by reading verses 2 and 3 of this 16th chapter of the Second Book of Kings, which tell us that

## Ahaz reigned over Judah

*"When Ahaz began to reign he was twenty years old, and he reigned in Jerusalem sixteen years, yet he did not do that which was right in the sight of the Lord his God, as his father David did, but walked in the way of the kings of Israel, and even caused his son to pass through the fire, according to the abominable practices of the nations whom the Lord cast out from before the children of Israel".*

Pekah reigned for twenty years before he was killed. In the seventeenth year of Pekah's reign in Israel, Ahaz king of Judah began to reign. Now, Ahaz was not a good king. Let's also read verse 4:

*"He sacrificed and burned incense in the high places, on the hills, and under every green tree".*

So he continued with the same bad behavior of the kings of Israel. He did terrible things like offering children as sacrifices to pagan gods. Generally children were sacrificed to Moloch or Baal. This practice showed how far a human being could be degraded, and that was precisely what Ahaz did. According to this verse 4, he went right into idolatry and pagan worship. Then we have the Syrian invasion of Israel and Judah. Let's read verse 5 of this chapter 16:

*"Then Rezin king of Syria and Pekah son of Remaliah king of Israel went up to Jerusalem to attack it and besiege Ahaz, but they could not take it".*

In the book of the prophet Isaiah 7 there is an extensive section on this subject. It is a very important section because it contains the prophecy of the virgin birth of the Lord Jesus Christ. Isaiah was prophesying to Ahaz, who would not listen to God. Then Isaiah challenged him to trust God. For example, in this chapter 7, verse 4, the Lord told Isaiah to speak to King Ahaz and say to him, "Take heed and be calm; do not be afraid, nor let your heart be troubled because of these two smoldering blighting capes, because of the fierce anger of Rezin and

Syria, and of the son of Remaliah". And then turning to verse 10 of the same chapter 7, of the book of Isaiah, we read until verse 12: "And the Lord spake unto Ahaz, saying, Ask thee a sign from the Lord thy God, and ask it either from beneath in the depths, or from above in the height. And Ahaz answered, I will not ask nor put the Lord to the test". In other words, the Lord brought these forces against Ahaz, because of his sins. Turning now to chapter 16 of the Second Book of Kings, which we are studying, let us see how Ahaz sought the help of Assyria and the Assyrians took Damascus. This move opened the door for Assyria to approach and would ultimately lead Israel, the northern kingdom, into captivity. Let us now read verses 7 and 8 of this chapter 16:

*"Then Ahaz sent ambassadors to Tiglath-pileser king of Assyria, saying, 'I am your servant and your son. Come up and defend me from the hand of the king of Syria and from the hand of the king of Israel, who have risen up against me. Ahaz took the silver and the gold that was in the house of the Lord and in the treasuries of the king's house, and sent a present to the king of Assyria".*

And so the Assyrians were bribed and came to the aid of King Ahaz, attacking Damascus in Syria and then taking the city. The high price of Assyria's help was vassalage. Ahaz had not what Isaiah had said, he did not believe the promise of the Lord.

Now, let's see what happened while Ahaz was in Damascus. Let's read verse 10:

*"Then King Ahaz went to Damascus to meet Tiglath-pileser king of Assyria. When king Ahaz saw the altar that was in Damascus, he sent to Uriah the priest the design and description of the altar, according to all the details".*

So there he saw an altar that impressed him greatly. And he wanted it to be copied so that he could build one and erect it in the temple of God. Meanwhile, the prophet Isaiah was prophesying against him and opposing what he was doing. He removed the altar of the Lord, which had been made according to the Lord's own instructions, and erected in its place, his own altar. He further plundered the house of God. Let us read verses 17 and 18 of this chapter 16 of the Second Book of Kings:

*"Then king Ahaz cut down the panels of the bases and removed the huge basin of water from above the bronze oxen that supported it and placed it on the stone floor. Because of the king of Assyria he removed from the temple of the Lord the porch for the Sabbath that they had built in the house, and the passage outside, the king's passage".*

Ahaz, therefore, stripped some precious ornaments and furnishings from the Temple for the benefit of the king of Assyria, showing his total lack of respect for the temple of the living and true God. Let us look at verses 19 and 20 of this chapter 16 of the Second Book of Kings:

*"And the rest of the acts which Ahaz did, are they not written in the book of the chronicles of the kings of Judah? King Ahaz slept with his fathers and was buried with them in the city of David. His son Hezekiah reigned in his stead.*

And so concludes this chapter 16, with the death of Ahaz and the fact that his son Hezekiah reigned after him. It was surprising that an ungodly man like Ahaz had a son like Hezekiah, who would be a good king and even lead a renewal movement, and whose reign we will read about in a later chapter.

## 2 Kings 17:1-6

This chapter presents the kingdom of Israel, the ten tribes of the northern kingdom, led into captivity. Let us enumerate the reasons why God allowed Israel to go into captivity. First, the people disobeyed God. We read in verse 13 of chapter 17: "And the Lord warned Israel and Judah by all the prophets and all the seers, saying, Turn ye from your evil ways, and keep my commandments and my statutes, according to all the laws which I commanded your fathers, which I sent unto you by my servants the prophets".

Secondly, Israel doubted God. We read in the next verse, verse 14 of this chapter 17: "But they obeyed not, but were obstinate, even as their fathers, who believed not in the Lord their God". And also, in the Second Book of Chronicles, chapter 36, verse 15, we read, "And the Lord, the God of their fathers, sent them warnings constantly by his messengers, for he had mercy on his people and on his dwelling place". And thirdly, God allowed Israel to go into captivity, because the people defied God. Verse 15, of this chapter 17 of the Second Book of Kings that we are studying, says: "And they rejected his statutes, and the covenant which he had made with their fathers, and the testimonies which he had commanded them, following after vanities, and making themselves vain, to imitate the nations that were round about them, though the Lord had commanded them that they should not do as they did". They defied God because they refused to keep the Sabbath years for 490 years. 2 Chronicles 36:21 says: "that the word of the Lord by the mouth of Jeremiah might be fulfilled, until the land had enjoyed rest; for all the time of its desolation it rested, until the seventy years were fulfilled".

The history of this nation of Israel is the same history of every individual. The first verses tell us about

## The kingdom of Hosea

In this chapter we come to the end of the line of descent, as far as the kingdom of Israel is concerned, when the 10 northern tribes were taken into captivity by Assyria. Verses 1 and 2 say:

> *"In the twelfth year of Ahaz king of Judah, Hoshea son of Elah began to reign in Samaria over Israel. He reigned nine years, and did evil in the sight of the Lord, though not like the kings of Israel who had been before him".*

Hosea was not as bad as Ahab and Jezebel, nor as Ahaziah, but still, he went quite far in his wickedness. And verses 3 to 5 say:

> *"Shalmaneser king of Assyria came up against Hoshea, who was made his servant and paid tribute to him. But the king of Assyria found out that Hoshea was plotting, for he had sent ambassadors to So, king of Egypt, and did not pay tribute to the king of Assyria, as he did every year, so the king of Assyria arrested him and locked him up in the prison house. Then the king of Assyria invaded the whole country and laid siege to Samaria, and was over it three years".*

Here we are introduced to Shalmaneser king of Assyria who conquered the northern kingdom and demanded the payment of tribute from the ten tribes. But when he discovered that King Hoshea had hatched a conspiracy against him and was not paying his tribute, he laid siege to Samaria, the city that had been built by Omri, Ahab's father, and where Ahab had built his palace. It was, no doubt, one of the most beautiful places in that land that was besieged by the king of Assyria. Let us now read verse 6 of this chapter 17 of the Second Book of Kings, where it is announced

## The captivity of Israel

> *"In the ninth year of Hoshea, the king of Assyria took Samaria and carried Israel captive to Assyria. He settled them in Halah, in Habor by the river Gozan, and in the cities of the Medes".*

There are those who say that the ten tribes are lost since they were taken into captivity. There are others who believe that the

Anglo-Saxon nations are descendants of those ten tribes. However, this idea constitutes a human deduction, totally foreign to the Word of God. For example, in the New Testament, the apostle James wrote in his letter the following, in chapter 1, verse 1: "James, a servant of God and of the Lord Jesus Christ, to the twelve tribes which are in the dispersion". Apparently, the apostle James did not believe that the tribes were lost. Now, when the Jews returned to their land, some of all the tribes returned. But, in reality, only a small percentage of the people returned. The Jews who were taken into captivity numbered several million and only about 65,000 returned to Palestine.

What happened in that kingdom was that, having turned away from God, it was left without spiritual foundations and its ruin was inevitable. So it also happens in the lives of people. In the parable of the two builders, in Luke 6:46-49, the Lord taught that the only sure foundation is found in His truth, in His teachings, in His Person. He alone is the object of true faith. The builder who built his house on earth, without a foundation to support it, saw that the house collapsed and was completely destroyed. The text says that "the ruin of that house was great". The people of Israel, as Moses said long before in his song recorded in Deuteronomy 32:15, abandoned the God who made them and despised the Rock of their salvation. Like that kingdom in our program today, many lives today are in a state of ruin and near collapse. But Jesus also spoke of another builder: the one who built his house on the foundation of the rock, and when the floods came and the water struck hard against that house, he could not move it. Dear reader, we invite you to rest your life on the Rock, on Jesus Christ, accepting by faith his work on the cross. Then you will stand firm against the onslaught of human wickedness, you will be able to face adversity with the power of God and, finally, you will be able to cross the threshold of death unmoved to enjoy eternal life.

# 2 Kings 17:7-18:16

Today we continue studying chapter 17 of the Second Book of Kings. And in the previous chapter, we talked about Shalmaneser, king of Assyria. And we saw that he conquered the northern kingdom and demanded tribute from the 10 tribes. But, when he discovered that King Hoshea had planned a conspiracy against him, he decided to besiege Samaria. And after 3 years, he took the ten northern tribes captive to Assyria. Now, as for Hosea, we said that he had not been as bad as Ahab and Jezebel, nor as Ahaziah, but he still went quite far in his wickedness. He tried to have good relations with Shalmaneser, king of Assyria, but he failed. Now Samaria was the city that Omri, Ahab's father, had built and where he had built a palace. It was one of the most beautiful places in all that land. Now, we said that there are those who say that the 10 tribes are lost, which is nothing more than a deduction, because in the Word of God there is not the slightest indication of it, nor is there any scientific basis to support it. For example, in the New Testament the apostle James wrote in his letter, chapter 1, verse 1: "James, a servant of God and of the Lord Jesus Christ, to the twelve tribes which are in the dispersion". Apparently, James did not believe that the tribes were lost. Now, when the Jews returned to their land, only a few of all the tribes returned. While the total number of Jews and Israelites who were taken into captivity numbered several million, only about 65,000 returned. Let's read verses 7 and 8 of this chapter 17 of the Second Book of Kings, to continue to consider

## Sins that caused the captivity of Israel

> "This happened because the children of Israel sinned against the Lord their God, who brought them out of the land of Egypt, from under the hand of Pharaoh king of Egypt. They worshiped other gods and walked in

*the statutes of the nations which the Lord had driven out from before the children of Israel, as well as in the statutes which the kings of Israel made".*

The Lord had been very patient with these people. Over a period of more than 200 years (after the division of the kingdom) the Lord had given them all kinds of opportunities, and plenty of time to turn to Him. But they did not. They continually indulged in idolatry. God's Word made it very clear that He sent them into captivity because they insisted on worshiping other gods. And we continue reading verses 9 and 10:

*"The children of Israel secretly did unseemly things against the Lord their God: they built for themselves high places in every city, from the watchtowers to the fortified cities, and they set up statues and images of Asherah on every high hill and under every leafy tree".*

In other words, pagan worship took place on the hills and under the trees. The Israelites indulged in gross immorality and tremendous debauchery. Let us continue with verses 11 and 12:

*"They burned incense in all the high places, after the manner of the nations which the Lord had removed from before them, and did very wicked things to provoke the Lord to anger. Moreover they served idols, concerning which the Lord had said unto them, Ye shall do no such thing".*

God had expelled from that land the heathen who dwelt there before, precisely because of their immorality and idolatry. Now, evidently God would not allow His own people to remain in that land and do the same. And He allowed Assyria to come and take them captive. And we read in verse 13:

*"Then the Lord warned Israel and Judah by all the prophets and all the seers, saying, Turn ye from your evil ways, and keep my commandments*

*and my statutes, according to all the laws which I commanded your fathers, which I sent unto you by my servants the prophets".*

God had sent the prophets Ahijah, Elijah, Micaiah, Elisha, Jonah, Amos and Hosea to the inhabitants of the northern kingdom of Israel. Now, to the southern kingdom of Judah, he had sent the prophets Shemaiah, Joel, Isaiah, Micah, Nahum, Habakkuk, Zephaniah and Jeremiah. Each prophet warned the people of both kingdoms about what would happen if they did not turn to God and forsake their wickedness. Verse 14 says here:

*"But they did not obey, but were as obstinate as their fathers, who did not believe in the Lord their God".*

The tribes were guilty of their own unbelief. The great sin of all mankind, Dear Reader, is that of not believing God. You and I live in a contemporary culture that has excluded God. He has no place in the educational system. And His will is of no interest in the centers of political decision making. And as a result, God will judge us just as He judged His people so long ago. Let us continue, reading verse 15 of this 17th chapter of the Second Book of Kings:

*"They rejected his statutes, the covenant which he had made with their fathers, and the testimonies which he had commanded them, following after vanities, and making themselves vain, because they imitated the nations which were round about them, though the Lord had commanded them that they should not do as they did".*

And the result was that the inhabitants of the northern kingdom were taken captive. And what would happen to the southern tribes? Let's read verse 19:

*"But even Judah kept not the commandments of the Lord their God, but walked in the customs which Israel had established".*

The kingdom of Judah did not benefit from the experience of the kingdom of Israel, as we shall see later. And verses 20 and 21 say:

> "Then the Lord cast away all the seed of Israel, and afflicted them, and delivered them into the hand of spoilers, until he had driven them from his presence. When he separated Israel from the house of David and they made Jeroboam son of Nebat king, Jeroboam turned Israel away from the way of the Lord and made them commit a great sin".

The fate of the southern kingdom would not really be any different from that of the north. Both kingdoms were guilty of rejecting their God. Both were guilty of doing evil in the sight of God. And although the inhabitants of Judah were not taken captive at this time, they too ended up being unfaithful to God. Here we are reminded of Jeroboam, who introduced calf worship in Israel. Let us now continue reading verses 22 and 23 of this chapter 17 of the Second Book of Kings:

> "And the children of Israel walked in all the sins which Jeroboam committed, and departed not from them, until the Lord removed Israel from his presence, as he had foretold by all the prophets, his servants. So Israel was carried away captive out of their land into Assyria, even unto this day".

The expression "to this day" means, of course, the time when the second book of Kings was written. We are now told that

## Israel's cities were repopulated with foreigners

Now, when the king of Assyria took the northern kingdom captive, he brought other peoples to inhabit the land. The region of the northern kingdom was called Samaria. The Samaritans of the New Testament would be the descendants of the settlers brought by the king of Assyria. And this would be the historical beginning of that people. And we continue reading verses 26 to 29:

*"And they said to the king of Assyria, The people whom thou hast carried away and placed in the cities of Samaria know not the law of the God of the land, and he hath cast lions among them, which slay them, because they know not the law of the God of the land. And the king of Assyria commanded: Take thither one of the priests whom ye brought thither from that place, that he may go and dwell there, and teach them the law of the God of the land. Then one of the priests whom they had carried away captive from Samaria went and dwelt in Bethel, and taught them how they should fear the Lord. But every nation made their own gods in the city where they dwelt, and set them up in the temples of the high places which they of Samaria had built".*

And this leads us to the end of the northern kingdom. The inhabitants of that land became a mixture of peoples, with the marriages of different races, with many marriages taking place between people of different races. And the ten tribes would never again form the northern kingdom. They are scattered today, but they are not lost. Let us now turn to

## 2 Kings 18:1-16

The theme of this chapter revolves around the renewal under King Hezekiah. This is such a remarkable section that it is not only recorded here in 2 Kings but also in 2 Chronicles and in the historical part of Isaiah's prophecy.

We have already seen, that the northern kingdom, that is the kingdom of Israel, was taken captive by Assyria and God gave three reasons that explained what happened. Israel disobeyed God, doubted God's Word and defied God. During the same period, the kingdom of Judah or the southern kingdom had a great king. It should be made clear that from this point on, we will be following the history of the southern kingdom or Judah, since the northern kingdom or Israel, was left out of the picture. The reason God did not send Judah into captivity at that time was that Judah had a few good kings who were responsible for a time of renewal.

Hezekiah was one of them. In fact, after King David, he was the best king that reigned over that people. Let us now read verses 1 to 3, of this chapter 18 of 2 Kings:

> *"In the third year of Hoshea son of Elah, king of Israel, Hezekiah son of Ahaz, king of Judah, began to reign. He was twenty-five years old when he began to reign, and he reigned twenty-nine years in Jerusalem. His mother's name was Abi, daughter of Zechariah. He did that which was right in the sight of the Lord, according to all that David his father had done".*

Hezekiah was the son of Ahaz. Now, Ahaz was a bad king, but he had a good son. And that leads us to believe that Hezekiah's mother was a good and godly woman, named Abi, who must have had a good influence on her son. Let us read verse 4, which starts to tell us about

## The renewal of Judah under King Hezekiah

> *"He took away the high places, broke the images, broke the Asherah symbols, and broke in pieces the brazen serpent that Moses had made, for until then the children of Israel burned incense to it; and he called it Nehushtan".*

Hezekiah was a remarkable man: he led his people to a renewal and began to attempt the eradication of idolatry from his people.

Now, this verse mentions the bronze serpent that Moses had lifted up in the wilderness, an incident we find in chapter 21 of the book of Numbers. What happened to that serpent that Moses lifted up? Well, they had kept it. Naturally it was a highly prized object and so it was kept in the temple. But, the day came when the children of Israel began to worship it. Instead of looking at it with faith, as their fathers had looked at it to save themselves, when they were bitten by the poisonous serpents in the wilderness as a judgment from God for their rebellion, they began to worship it. But, now this same serpent had become a stumbling block. The people had forgotten its meaning. The serpent was a symbol of Christ, as we see in the gospel according to John, chapter 3, verses 14 and 15, where we read: "And as Moses lifted up the serpent in the wilderness, even so must the Son of man be lifted up, that whosoever believeth in him should not perish, but have everlasting life". The bronze serpent, then, was a symbol that was fulfilled by Christ. But, now we have the case of these people who have begun to worship this serpent, instead of worshipping God.

In studying the seven churches of Asia Minor, in the book of Revelation, we observe that in the city of Pergamum, they worshipped the serpent. And it seems that the children of Israel were doing the same thing. They were burning incense to the bronze serpent. Now, what did the king do? Hezekiah broke it in pieces to get rid of it.

There is a spiritual lesson here. There have been certain organizations, certain movements, and methods that God has used in the past. But unfortunately, people were not aware that God had finished using them and have refused to discard them. And we are sure that in their day, they were very useful and served a great purpose. They accomplished much, but they became inadequate for the present circumstances. Yet they were sacralized, becoming something like that bronze serpent. But, then came the day when God ended them. Therefore we need to have the spiritual sensitivity to evaluate the customs or methods, in short, everything that was temporary, passing and needs to be discarded, adapted to the new situations, renewed and, on the other hand, what is permanent, essential, that transcends in time and circumstances. Well, let us now continue reading verses 5 and 6 of this chapter 18 of the Second Book of Kings:

> "In the Lord, the God of Israel, he put his hope. Among all the kings of Judah there was none like him, before or since, for he followed the Lord and did not turn away from him, but kept the commandments which the Lord commanded Moses".

If there was none like Hezekiah before or since, then we must conclude that he was extraordinary. He was on an equal footing with David. He was a great king whom God used mightily. That is why the account of his life, we find it in three books of the Old Testament. We find it in the Second Book of Kings, in the Second Book of Chronicles and in the Book of the prophet Isaiah. Let's continue reading now, verses 7 through 10, of this chapter 18 of the Second Book of Kings, which describes

## The first invasion of Judah

> "The Lord was with him, and wherever he went, he prospered. Hezekiah rebelled against the king of Assyria and did not serve him. He also defeated the Philistines as far as Gaza and its borders, from the watchtowers to the fortified city. In the fourth year of King Hezekiah, which was the seventh year of Hoshea son of Elah, king of Israel, Shalmaneser king of Assyria came up against Samaria and besieged it. At the end of three years they took it. In the sixth year of Hezekiah, which was the ninth year of Hoshea king of Israel, Samaria was taken".

Hezekiah was a brave king. Under his rule, Judah rebelled against Assyria and also defeated the Philistines. During the sixth year of Hezekiah's reign, Shalmaneser, king of Assyria took Samaria. And the northern kingdom was defeated. Now, there was nothing, not even a barbed wire fence between Assyria and Judah. And King Hezekiah found himself in a bind. And we continue reading in verses 11 and 12 of this Second Book of Kings:

> *"The king of Assyria carried Israel captive into Assyria, and settled them in Halah by the river Gozan in Habor, and in the cities of the Medes, because they had not hearkened to the voice of the Lord their God, but had broken his covenant, and had not hearkened nor done all that Moses the servant of the Lord had commanded".*

We have just read an account of the captivity of Israel. Let us continue reading verses 13 and 14:

> *"In the fourteenth year of Hezekiah the king Sennacherib king of Assyria came up against all the fenced cities of Judah and took them. Then Hezekiah king of Judah sent to the king of Assyria who was at Lachish, saying, 'I have sinned; leave my country, and whatever you impose on me I will accept. So the king of Assyria imposed on Hezekiah king of Judah a tribute of nine thousand nine hundred pounds of silver, and nine hundred and ninety pounds of gold".*

Hezekiah tried to rebel against Assyria, but was unsuccessful. And he admitted that he had made a mistake by allying himself with other nations against Assyria. So, then he would have to pay tribute. Let's read verses 15 and 16:

> *"Hezekiah therefore delivered up all the silver that was in the house of the Lord and in the treasuries of the king's house. On that occasion Hezekiah took away the gold from the doors of the temple of the Lord and from the chiciales which King Hezekiah himself had overlaid with gold, and gave it to the king of Assyria".*

In this program we have seen how a historical souvenir such as the bronze serpent, was turned by the people into an object of worship, forgetting that it had been a symbol that pointed to God and His power to restore all those who in the ancient incident in the desert had been bitten by the serpent. And it seems that the tendency towards idolatry has continued through the centuries, with peculiar characteristics in each epoch of history, encompassing everything that, becoming an obsession, removes God from the minds of human beings. Therefore, we need to remember the wilderness incident, in the light of our present situation. As with the snakebite, sin and wickedness have permanently wounded mankind. The effects of the poison have been transmitted from generation to generation and its effects are evident in the ills that afflict the individual and society. Therefore, the words of the Gospel of John 3, quoted above, are still valid: "As Moses lifted up the serpent in the wilderness, even so must the Son of man, that is, Jesus Christ, be lifted up, that whoever believes in him should not perish but have eternal life. Just as those travelers in the desert had to look to the symbol that God had established to save them, we invite you, dear reader, to direct a look of faith to the Lord Jesus Christ, because he is the only remedy to avoid perdition, to imprint on your existence a life of authentic quality, and the only way to receive eternal life.

# 2 Kings 18:17-19:32

We continue our study of chapter 18 of the Second Book of Kings. And in the previous chapter, we talked about king Hezekiah. And we said that he was an extraordinary king, because neither before him nor after him, was there another like him among all the kings of Judah. He was a great king whom God used mightily. And we said that for that reason, we find the account of his life in three books of the Old Testament: in the Second Book of Kings, in the Second Book of Chronicles and in the prophecy of Isaiah. We also saw that Hezekiah tried, unsuccessfully, to rebel against Assyria. And for that reason, he would have to pay tribute. Now, Sennacherib, tried to terrorize the southern kingdom, or Judah and threatened the city of Jerusalem. And we saw how Hezekiah gave up all the silver that was found in the house of the Lord and in the treasuries of the royal house. He also took away the gold from the doors of the temple and their frames, which he himself had overlaid with gold, and gave it all to the king of Assyria. Let's read verses 17 to 21 of this chapter 18 of the Second Book of Kings, to consider

## The second invasion of Judah by Sennacherib

> *"Then the king of Assyria sent against King Hezekiah the chief of the armies, the chief of the eunuchs, and the chief butler over a great army, and they went up from Lachish to Jerusalem to attack it. When they arrived, they encamped by the aqueduct of the upper pool, on the way to the Washer's field. Then they called for the king, and Eliakim the son of Hilkiah, the steward, and Shebna the scribe, and Joah the son of Asaph the recorder, went out to meet them. And the chief butler said unto them, Say now unto Hezekiah, Thus saith the great king of Assyria, What confidence is this whereon thou leanest? Thou sayest (but they are empty*

*words): Counsel have I, and strength for war. But on what do you trust, that you have rebelled against me? I see that you trust in this staff of splintered reed, in Egypt, which if one leans on it, it sticks in him and pierces his hand. Such is Pharaoh, king of Egypt, to all who trust in him".*

Sennacherib tried to terrorize Hezekiah by threatening Jerusalem with a large army. He sent a delegation to speak to Hezekiah. The king, in turn, sent his delegates. The message that Sennacherib sent to Hezekiah was a direct pagan challenge against God. Knowing that Hezekiah was expecting help from Egypt, his chief cupbearer ridiculed Egypt by comparing it to a splintered reed that if one leaned on it, it would stick in and pierce his hand. It was like telling him that he could not expect any help from Egypt. And then he tried to remove the second support. Let us continue reading verse 22:

*"If ye say unto me, We trust in the Lord our God, is not this he whose high places and altars Hezekiah hath taken away, and hath said unto Judah and Jerusalem, Ye shall worship before this altar in Jerusalem?"*

It seems here that Sennacherib was confused. When Hezekiah removed the high places, Sennacherib believed that he was removing the altars to the living and true God. He did not understand that Hezekiah was removing pagan altars and idols from the land, and that his action was an act of obedience, not sacrilege. The Jews worshipped God only at a single altar in Jerusalem. They approached God only by means of a blood sacrifice. However, it seemed to Sennacherib that Hezekiah had cast off his God when he needed him most. And we continue reading verse 23 of this chapter 18 of the Second Book of Kings:

*"Now, then, I beg you to make a bargain with my lord, the king of Assyria: I will give you two thousand horses if you will get horsemen for them".*

This was an insult and a strong expression of contempt for Judah's military power. Now, it was true that God used foreign nations to punish His people. Let us continue reading here verses 25 and 26:

> "Have I now come to this place to destroy it without the LORD? The Lord said to me, 'Go up to this land and destroy it. Then Eliakim the son of Hilkiah and Shebna and Joah said to the chief butler, "Speak to your servants, we pray you, in Aramaic, for we understand it, and do not speak to us in the language of Judah in the hearing of the people on the wall.

Now the Jews were lined up on the city wall of Jerusalem, watching all that was going on. The officers of Judah requested that any conversation that took place, be done in the language of the Syrians, to avoid a negative effect on the people. But the Syrian chief cupbearer was demoralizing the troops and said here in verses 28 to 32:

> "Then the chief butler stood up and cried with a loud voice in the language of Judah, Hear the word of the great king, the king of Assyria. Thus saith the king, Let not Hezekiah deceive you, for he cannot deliver you out of my hand. Let not Hezekiah make you trust in the Lord, saying, Surely the Lord will deliver us, and this city shall not be given into the hand of the king of Assyria. Hearken not unto Hezekiah: for thus saith the king of Assyria, Make ye peace with me, and yield yourselves unto me: let every man eat of his vine and of his fig tree, and drink ye every man the water of his well, until I come and bring you into a land like unto your own, a land of corn and wine, a land of bread and vineyards, a land of olives, of oil and honey. You shall live and not die. Do not listen to Hezekiah, for he deceives you when he says, The Lord will deliver us".

The Assyrian delegation tried to persuade the Jews to surrender. It repeated that neither Hezekiah nor God could help them. It told them that their lives would be saved only by surrender. And that even if they were deported, they would be taken to a land as wonderful as theirs.

And he continued the cupbearer speaking here in verses 33 to 35 and said:

> "Have any of the gods of the nations delivered their land out of the hand of the king of Assyria? Where is the god of Hamath and Arphad? Where is the god of Sepharvaim, of Hena, and of Ivah? Were these gods able to deliver Samaria out of my hands? What god among all the gods of these lands has delivered their land out of my hands, that the Lord may deliver Jerusalem out of my hands?"

For the cupbearer this was an overwhelming and unanswerable argument. It was true that no god had delivered his people from the power of the king of Assyria. Of course he did not know that the gods of the other nations were not really gods, while the living and true God is the "Lord of the whole earth". And verse 36 of this 18th chapter of 2 Kings says:

> "But the people held their peace, and answered him not a word; for the king had given a commandment, saying, Answer him not".

This section therefore concludes with the report of the delegates of King Hezekiah, on the negotiations with the ambassadors or delegates of the Syrian emperor.

## 2 Kings 19:1-32

In this chapter King Hezekiah turned to God and to the prophet Isaiah. The following events are highlighted. In great distress, he asked Isaiah to pray for the people of Israel in the face of the Assyrian threat. Isaiah, for his part, encouraged them. Sennacherib sent a blasphemous letter to Hezekiah. We have then, the prayer of Exequias, Isaiah's prophecy against Sennacherib, the death of the Assyrians by an angel, and the death of Sennacherib by his own sons.

Hezekiah came to the throne in times of great distress, upheaval and uncertainty. The northern kingdom had been taken captive by Assyria. At this time the Assyrian army had arrived at the very entrance to Jerusalem. This was enough to frighten Hezekiah. And besides, the chief cupbearer and trusted man of the king of Assyria, stood outside the wall spreading all kinds of taunts and insults. He boasted about the great things that Assyria would do against Jerusalem and ridiculed the idea that God could deliver them. Poor Hezekiah almost fainted at all this, which was natural because Hezekiah was still learning to turn to the Lord and trust in Him. Let us read, then, the first verse of this chapter 19, where we see that in the first place,

## Hezekiah sought God's help

*"When King Hezekiah heard it, he tore his clothes, covered himself with rough garments, and went into the house of the Lord".*

Rending his clothes and putting on rough garments indicated Hezekiah's deep sorrow and affliction. Let us note that he went to the temple of the Lord. And, by the way, it is a good place to go when you are in a state of depression. It's the right time to go to God. And we continue reading verse 2:

*"And he sent Eliakim the butler, and Shebna the scribe, and the elders of the priests, covered with rough garments, to see Isaiah the prophet the son of Amoz".*

We wonder if you, dear reader, have observed any parallels between this situation and the times in which we live. Although we believe that many consider that we are living in a highly advanced and humanitarian age, with a Western and Christian culture, and that the nation of King Hezekiah was uncivilized, primitive with elements of paganism. However, in the midst of all the overwhelming personal, family and social problems we are facing, have you ever heard of any leader turning to God to know His will or to ask for His help in overcoming any emergency or conflict situation? Surely the answer will be no. And yet, despite the abundance of specialized experts in all areas, the situation tends to worsen and it seems increasingly difficult to harmonize dissenting opinions or to control the growing aggressiveness among the members of a society so sophisticated in its organization. Our only hope, Dear Reader, is to turn to God in this dark and threatening hour we face in history.

Hezekiah had enough judgment to turn to God in his hour of need. Let us continue, now, reading verses 3 through 5 of this chapter 19 of the Second Book of Kings:

*"That they might say to him: Thus said Hezekiah: This day is a day of trouble, and of rebuke, and of blasphemy, because the children are about to be born, and she that beareth is without strength. Perhaps the Lord, your God, will hear all the words of the chief cupbearer, whom the king of the Assyrians, your lord, has sent to blaspheme against the living God and to insult with words, which the Lord, your God, has heard. Therefore lift up a prayer for the remnant that still remain. Then the servants of king Hezekiah came to see Isaiah".*

We see that Hezekiah said: "Perhaps the Lord your God will hear all the words of the chief butler". Note that he did not say, "Our God," but your God. Poor Hezekiah! Perhaps he did not know God well, but he had sense enough to appeal to Him in such a distressing time as this. He really had no alternative but to turn directly to God. And Isaiah answered him in verses 6 and 7:

*"And he said unto them, Thus shall ye say unto your lord, Thus saith the LORD, Fear not for the words which thou hast heard, wherewith the servants of the king of Assyria have blasphemed against me. Behold, I will put a spirit in him, he shall hear a rumor, he shall return to his own land, and there I will cause him to fall by the sword".*

This prophecy was literally fulfilled. Now, let's look at the encouragement Isaiah gave the king. He told him not to worry about him: he was a braggart who boasted and blasphemed. In time, God would deal with him.

Dear reader, if only we would learn to let God take care of our enemies! Difficulties and problems arise when we try to deal with this type of situation in our own strength, and according to our own judgment, and we turn away from faith and trust in God, so that He does not intervene on our behalf and we will be disappointed. Let us read verses 8 and 9 of this chapter 19 of the Second Book of Kings, to begin to consider

## The threatening letter

> *"The chief cupbearer returned and found the king of Assyria fighting against Libnah, for he heard that he had left Lachish. There the king of Syria learned that Tirhaca, king of Ethiopia, had gone out to make war against him, and he sent ambassadors back to Hezekiah saying"*

The chief cupbearer who had returned to his lord found him involved in a war against Libnah. And a threatening action of the king of Ethiopia prevented him from returning to attack Jerusalem immediately. So he sent Hezekiah a letter of warning. What he told him is expressed in verses 10 to 13:

> *Thus shall you say to Hezekiah king of Judah, 'Let not the God in whom you trust deceive you, saying, "Jerusalem shall not be given into the hand of the king of Assyria. You have heard what the kings of Assyria have done to all the lands which they have destroyed. Will you escape? Did their gods deliver the nations which my fathers destroyed, that is, Gozan, Haran, Resef, and the children of Eden who were in Telasar? Where is the king of Hamath, the king of Arphad, and the king of the city of Sepharvaim, of Hena, and of Ivah?"*

It was an unsettling message. The king of Assyria had moved every obstacle out of his way. How did Hezekiah think he was going to escape? Verse 14 says:

> "Hezekiah took the letter from the hands of the ambassadors. When he had read it, he went up to the house of the Lord and spread it before the Lord".

Dear reader, we need to spread our problems before the Lord, just as Hezekiah did. Since the day we started broadcasting this program The Fountain of Life, we have received many very special letters. We have been able to lay them before the Lord in prayer, letting Him solve the problems, because we cannot do it ourselves. He is a specialist in this. Hezekiah, then, acted wisely when he spread the letters before the Lord. And we continue reading verses 15 and 16 of this chapter 19 of the Second Book of Kings, which begin to present

## Hezekiah's prayer

> "Then Hezekiah prayed before the Lord, saying, 'Lord, God of Israel, who dwells between the cherubim, you alone are God of all the kingdoms of the earth. You made heaven and earth. Incline your ear, O Lord, and hear; open your eyes, O Lord, and see. Hear the words that Sennacherib has sent to tell me to blaspheme the living God".

Let us observe how Hezekiah approached God. Have you ever felt that God does not listen to you? This is how Hezekiah felt. Let's continue listening to him in verses 17 and 18:

> "It is true, O Lord, that the kings of Assyria have destroyed the nations and their lands, and that they have cast their gods into the fire, because they were not gods, but the work of men's hands, of wood or stone, and therefore they destroyed them".

What the chief cupbearer of Syria had said was true. He was not boasting when he said that Assyria had overcome all the obstacles that came its way and had already cast the idols of other nations into the fire. And the prayer ended with the appeal we find in verse 19, which goes like this:

> "Now therefore, O Lord our God, save us, I pray thee, from their hands, that all the kingdoms of the earth may know that thou alone, O Lord, art God".

And then let us read verse 20, where it begins

## God's response

> "Then Isaiah the son of Amoz sent to Hezekiah, saying, 'Thus says the Lord, the God of Israel, "I have heard what you asked me concerning Sennacherib king of Assyria.

It is important to note that God said that He was listening to Hezekiah as he prayed. And He went on to say in verses 21 and 22:

> "This is the word which the Lord hath spoken concerning him, The virgin, O daughter of Zion, despiseth thee, she mocketh thee; at thy back the daughter of Jerusalem shaketh her head: whom hast thou insulted, and against whom hast thou blasphemed, against whom hast thou lifted up thy voice, and lifted up thine eyes haughtily? Against the Holy One of Israel.

Here God's intention to destroy that army of Assyria is emphasized. And the answer continued in verses 23 and 24:

> "Through your messengers you have insulted the Lord and said, 'With the multitude of my chariots I have gone up to the heights of the mountains, to the most inaccessible of Lebanon; I will cut down its tall cedars, its choicest cypresses; I will lodge in its remotest places, in the forest

*of its fertile fields. I have dug and drunk the strange waters, I have dried up with the soles of my feet all the rivers of Egypt".*

God here repeated the boastful words of the king of Assyria, that the mountains would not stop him, nor would the deserts, for he would dig wells for water. Nor would the rivers be an obstacle, for he would find ways to dry them up.

Now God addressed the proud king of Assyria. He told him that the rise and fall of the nations was His doing. Isaiah had written earlier in chapter 10:5 of his prophecy, that God said that Assyria was the stick with which He in His wrath punished, and the rod which He used when He was angry. And, returning to our text in this 19th chapter of 2 Kings, let us read verses 25 and 26:

*"But have you never heard that from ancient times I have done it, and that from the days of old I have devised it? For now I have caused it to come: You will cause desolations, and reduce the fortified cities to heaps of rubble. Their inhabitants, helpless, were dismayed and confounded; they became as the grass of the field, as the green herb, as the hay of the housetops, which withers before it ripens".*

That is, the victims of Assyria were unable to offer effective resistance because it was God who filled their hearts with fear. And verses 27 and 28 add:

*"I have known your situation, all your movements, and your anger against me. Because you have been angry with me, because your arrogance has come up to my ears, I will put my hook in your nose and my bridle on your lips, and I will turn you back the way by which you came".*

Here God set forth his intention to stop the invader and send him back the way he had come. And now let us read verse 29:

> "This I will give you for a sign, Hezekiah: This year ye shall eat that which shall spring of his own, and the second year that which shall spring of his own. In the third year you shall sow and reap, you shall plant vineyards and eat the fruit of them".

The Lord addressed Hezekiah here. Apparently, the presence of the Assyrian army had caused the farmers around Jerusalem not to sow their land. God promised that with the wheat that would spring up on its own they would have enough to eat, and even in the third year they could sow and reap their harvest in peace. For King Sennacherib of Assyria would not be around to destroy the harvest. And we continue reading verses 30 to 32:

> "Whatever has escaped, whatever is left of the house of Judah, shall again take root underneath and bear fruit above. For out of Jerusalem shall come forth a remnant, and out of Mount Zion those who are saved. The zeal of the Lord of hosts will do this. Therefore thus saith the Lord concerning the king of Assyria; He shall not enter into this city, neither shall he shoot arrows into it; neither shall he meet it with a shield, nor set up a bulwark against it".

Isaiah was making a very bold statement, but it was the Word of the Lord. Surely the people of Jerusalem would wonder if Isaiah was a true prophet. When Isaiah made a prophecy of distant fulfillment in time, such as, for example, that the virgin would conceive and bear a son, people might speculate as to when such a prophecy would be fulfilled. And it would not be fulfilled until the birth of Christ, some seven hundred years later; so no one who heard this prophecy would be there to verify its fulfillment. But in our story today, Isaiah was uttering a prophecy about a local situation, the fulfillment of which they would see within a few days.

There was the Assyrian army camped outside the gates of Jerusalem. That army had overthrown all opposition and was feared in the ancient world. At that time God was declaring through Isaiah that they would not besiege the city of Jerusalem and that they would not even shoot a single arrow into the city.

Let us think that there were about 185,000 soldiers around the walls of Jerusalem. One would expect that among so many, there would be at least one soldier ready to shoot an arrow over the walls. If that had happened, then it would have been evident that Isaiah was not a true prophet of God. For God had said, through Isaiah, that not a single arrow would fall on the city. That, then, would be the way the people of that time would know that he was a true prophet of God.

Today we ended with an image of God's majesty. Acting as a sovereign and just judge, we saw him act to protect a people and stop an invincible invading army with his power. But we have also seen him as a merciful and patient God, who reveals himself to human beings in many ways, according to their historical moment and condition. That is why He sent His Son Jesus Christ, the Prince of Peace, into the world with a message of salvation, so that those who are far from Him may change direction, turn to Him, and believe in Him.

# 2 Kings 19:33-20:19

We continue our study of chapter 19 of the Second Book of Kings. And in the previous chapter, we were considering God's second answer to King Hezekiah, through the prophet Isaiah. And we saw that God answered Hezekiah's prayer and sent the prophet Isaiah to tell Hezekiah that his prayer had been answered and that God would destroy the army of Assyria. We also saw that God reproached Assyria for its boastfulness. Then, the Lord addressed Hezekiah and described to him a period of ample harvest of 3 years. In other words, they could enjoy what Assyria had sown, and would only have to sow themselves in the third year. Sennacherib and his army would no longer be there to harvest the fruit. In other words, God was telling Hezekiah that the city of Jerusalem would evade destruction and that the people who would survive the invasion would increase in number. God was predicting the failure of Sennacherib's attack. The strategy and the devastating tactics of the Assyrians would not succeed this time against Jerusalem. In other words, the king of Assyria would not succeed in his effort against God's people.

Many nations had fallen before this terrible nation, and the Assyrians were feared throughout the ancient world. They had reached the wall of Jerusalem and had withdrawn. Now God says that the Assyrians would be there again, but, that it would not be possible for them to encircle or besiege the city. The fact is that they would not even shoot a single arrow at the city. Now, think about this for a moment. There would be about two hundred thousand soldiers around the wall of Jerusalem. Out of that many men, one soldier might have had a great desire to shoot an arrow over the wall. But, if a single man were to shoot an arrow over the wall of Jerusalem, he would prove that Isaiah was not a true prophet of God. But, we will see here that Isaiah was indeed a true prophet. Let us read verses 33 and 34 of this chapter 19, of the Second Book of Kings, in which Isaiah continued to speak on behalf of the Lord:

> *"By the same way that he came, he shall return, and shall not come into this city, saith the Lord. For I will defend this city to save it, for my own sake, and for my servant David's sake".*

God does many things for His name's sake. He did many things for David's sake. David would have a descendant born of a virgin, and that would be the Lord Jesus Christ. And God does many things for love of Him. God saves sinners who trust in Him as their personal Savior. And when a believer prays to the Father in Jesus' name, God the Father responds out of love for Christ. So, let's continue with verse 35:

> *"And it came to pass the same night that the angel of the Lord went out and slew in the camp of the Assyrians an hundred and eighty-five thousand men. And when they arose in the morning, they were all dead bodies".*

Those inhabitants of the city that rose up, found in the enemy camp a desolate panorama. Let us read the final verses of this chapter 19 of the Second Book of Kings, verses 36 and 37, which describe how:

## Sennacherib was killed by his sons

> *"Then Sennacherib king of Assyria departed and returned to Nineveh, where he stayed. And it came to pass that while he was worshiping in the temple of Nisroch, his god, his sons Adrammelech and Sarezer smote him with the sword and fled to the land of Ararat. And Esar-haddon, his son, reigned in his stead".*

Here we see that his death was the result of a palace plot. It is interesting that the prophecy concerning Assyria was literally fulfilled at that time.

## 2 Kings 20:1-19

And in this chapter, the theme revolves around Hezekiah's illness and his healing. The following events are recounted: Hezekiah prayed and his life was prolonged. The sun went back 10 degrees, as a sign of that promise. The prophet Isaiah predicted the Babylonian captivity, and finally, Hezekiah died, and Manasseh, his son, ascended the throne of Judah. As we will see later in our study, Hezekiah became ill and believed that the hour of his death had come. He prayed that the Lord would heal him, and God heard his prayer. Now, we believe that this is a case that perhaps it would have been better if he had died at the appointed time. For we shall see, that after his improvement, Hezekiah committed three foolish acts, and they were as follows. First, he allowed the ambassadors of Babylon, to see all his treasures. Second, he begat Manasseh, who became the worst of all kings. And thirdly, Hezekiah's heart was filled with pride. Let us keep in mind that Hezekiah was an extraordinary king. After David, there was no other like him. He did what was right in the sight of the Lord according to all that David his father did. That was God's testimony about him. Let's read verse 1, then, to consider

## Hezekiah's illness

*"In those days Hezekiah fell sick unto death. And Isaiah the prophet the son of Amoz went to him and said to him, 'Thus says the Lord: Set thy house in order, for thou shalt die, thou shalt not live any more".*

This sickness of Hezekiah is related three times in the Scriptures. We have it here in this 20th chapter of the Second Book of Kings; also in the 32nd chapter of the Second Book of Chronicles, and finally, in the 38th chapter of Isaiah's prophecy. Now, each account gives us an additional detail to the total picture. We believe it was a difficult task for Isaiah to communicate a death sentence to King Hezekiah. However, the death sentence is upon each of us, although we do not know the day and hour of its fulfillment. The writer to the Hebrews said in chapter 9, verse 27: "And as it is appointed unto men once to die, and after this the judgment". This is a divine quote. Even if each of us knew the exact moment we are going to die, would we not change our way of living? In the end, we must live knowing that this will be the final goal.

Let's continue reading the story of Hezekiah's experience. Let's read verses 2 and 3:

> *"Then he turned his face to the wall, and prayed thus unto the Lord, I pray thee, O Lord, I pray thee, remember, I have walked faithfully before thee, and with an honest heart, that I have done the things that please thee. And Hezekiah wept bitterly".*

We think we understand how Hezekiah felt. Suppose you were told that you had a serious illness and neither you nor the doctor knew what the outcome would be. (Dr. McGee, the author of these Bible studies, said that throughout his ministry he has visited those suffering from cancer. He was able to understand how they would feel but, he said, it never crossed his mind that one day he, too, would suffer from it. He confessed that he was stunned when the doctor informed him that he had the disease. He could not believe it. When he finally had to accept it, the doctors could not give him any assurance that they could heal him completely. He added that such an experience makes one change one's values and priorities, and that he then desired to live in a way that would please the Lord).

Continuing our story, Hezekiah realized that only God could help him. When he turned to Him in prayer, he reminded the Lord that he had lived before Him doing what pleased Him. Now, let's look at what God did. Let's read verses 4 through 6:

*And before Isaiah went out into the midst of the court, the Lord spoke to Isaiah and said to him, "Go back and tell Hezekiah, the prince of my people, 'Thus says the Lord, the God of David your father, "I have heard your prayer, I have seen your tears, and I am going to heal you; within three days you shall go up to the house of the Lord. I will add fifteen years to your days, and will deliver you and this city out of the hand of the king of Assyria. I will defend this city for my own sake and for my servant David's sake.*

The Lord had seen Hezekiah's tears. And we are sure that He had seen his tears, and mine. And the Lord informed the king that he would be healed and that his life would be prolonged for about fifteen more years. Let us now read verse 7, which announces to us

## Hezekiah's recovery

*Isaiah said, "Take a lump of figs. They took it, put it on the sore and it healed".*

God used natural means to heal Hezekiah. But, he also uses supernatural means. The apostle James said in chapter 5 of his letter, verses 14 and 15: "Is anyone sick among you? Let him call for the elders of the church, that they may pray for him, anointing him with oil in the name of the Lord. And the prayer of faith will save the sick person, and the Lord will raise him up; and if he has committed sins, they will be forgiven him".

Of course, these indications in no way exclude the intervention of the physician. The general principle is that church leaders should also be called upon, so that they can pray for the sick person.

We believe that his illness may well have been cancer. God announced to him the prolongation of his life and at the same time told him to use a natural product such as fig paste on his sore. It is evident that God is sovereign to heal directly, or to use natural therapeutic means. Treatments and medicines are not in contradiction with God's intervention. Let us not forget that when we entrust ourselves to Him, we trust Him to control the process of our recovery. Let us now continue reading verse 8 of this chapter 20 of the Second Book of Kings:

> *"And Hezekiah had said to Isaiah, What sign shall I have that the Lord will heal me, and that within three days I shall go up to the house of the Lord?"*

Hezekiah asked for a sign to show that his life would be prolonged. But let us remember that it will not always be the Lord's will to prolong a life. In the early church for example, James was a martyr, executed by Herod. On the other hand, Peter was released from prison. Now, we do not know why one was released, while the other had to die as a martyr. All this depends on God's providence and we want His will to be done. We should pray that God humbles us and helps us to accept His will, so that our desires are in harmony with His purposes for us. But, on the other hand, we believe that we can tell God what we think or desire regarding a given situation. And then, we can rest confidently knowing that He is in control of our particular situation. Okay, let's continue with verses 9 through 11 of this 20th chapter of the Second Book of Kings:

> *"Isaiah answered, This sign shalt thou have from the Lord, that the Lord will do as he hath said, Shall the shadow go forward ten degrees, or shall it go backward ten degrees? Hezekiah answered, It is easy for the shadow to decline ten degrees, but not for the shadow to go back ten degrees. Then*

*Isaiah the prophet cried to the Lord, and he caused the shadow to go back the ten degrees that it had advanced in Ahaz's watch".*

Here it could be steps or rungs of a ladder that led up to the terrace built by King Ahaz, which God used on this occasion to give a sign to Hezekiah, or a sundial. Now, after his healing, let us read verses 12 and 13 of this chapter 20 of the Second Book of Kings, for the account will make us see

## Hezekiah's folly

*"At that time Merodach-baladan son of Baladan, king of Babylon, sent messengers with letters and presents to Hezekiah, for he had heard that Hezekiah had fallen sick. Hezekiah waited on them and showed them all his treasure house, the silver and gold, the spices and precious ointments, his store of weapons, and all that was in his treasuries. There was nothing left that Hezekiah did not show them, both in his house and in all his dominions".*

Now, this was a kind gesture on the part of the Babylonian royalty, they sent Hezekiah a gift and a message wishing him well. Then Hezekiah responded by doing something foolish. He let the Babylonian ambassadors see all the treasures that Solomon had accumulated. The riches of the world were there, which was not public knowledge. But Hezekiah was generous. But, God, was not pleased with this act of Hezekiah and let's see what He said to him. Let's read verses 14 to 17:

*Then Isaiah the prophet went to King Hezekiah and said to him, "Where did these men come from, and what did they say to you? Hezekiah said to him, 'They came from a far country, from Babylon. Isaiah asked him again, What did they see in your house? Hezekiah answered, "They saw everything that was in my house. There was nothing left in my treasures that I did not show them. Then Isaiah said to Hezekiah, Hear this word from the Lord, The days are coming when all that is in your house and all that your fathers have treasured up to this day will be carried away to Babylon, with nothing left, says the Lord".*

Hezekiah organized an excursion for the ambassadors from Babylon. He received them with full honors and showed them everything. These visitors, of course, made an inventory of all the riches, and took it back to Babylon to wait for the right time when they would need gold. Then, when they needed more riches, they would know where to find them. And the Lord continued speaking through the prophet Isaiah, and said in verses 18 and 19:

*"And some of the children that come out of you, which you have begotten, they shall take them to be castrated servants in the palace of the king of Babylon. Then Hezekiah said to Isaiah, The word which thou hast spoken from the Lord is good. For he thought, At least in my days there will be peace and safety".*

Isaiah told Hezekiah what would happen to his descendants. They would be taken captive and become servants in the palace of the king of Babylon. But, we do not like the answer Hezekiah gave Isaiah. In reality, it did not constitute a confession of sin. He wanted rather to enjoy peace in his own time, and showed no interest in his offspring upon whom the coming catastrophe would fall.

The last two verses of this chapter 20 of the Second Book of Kings tell us about the death of Hezekiah, an event that we will leave for our consideration in our next chapter because our time for today has already concluded. Today we have paid attention to the dramatic announcement that the prophet Isaiah, on behalf of God, communicated to King Hezekiah, telling him that he was going to die. His words were blunt. He told him: "Put your house in order, for you are going to die". This incident reminds us of a parable that Jesus told in the New Testament, specifically, in the Gospel of Luke

12:16-21. A rich man, whose land had produced a great harvest, began to think about where he would store the harvested fruits. The struggle to acquire material goods was evidently the only concern of his life. His existence was limited to hard work and the accumulation of wealth. So he came to the conclusion that it would be best to tear down his barns and build larger ones so that he could store all his harvest and the rest of his goods. Thus, in his thoughts, he tried to enjoy in advance the idea of being assured of a future of many years of security and prosperity. But one day God announced to him: "You fool, you are going to die this very night: for whom will be what you have stored up?" And the conclusion of the parable was: "This happens to the man who accumulates riches for himself, but is not rich before God". The tragedy of that person was that it never crossed his mind that his life was fleeting, that he was spiritually dead, and that he would face death unprepared to stand before God. Let us remember the warning of the Biblical quotation we presented at the beginning of our program, from the writer to the Hebrews, chapter 9, verse 27: "And as it is appointed unto men once to die, and after this the judgment". How different is the situation of the Christian! The Christian, in whom Christ dwells, enjoys a unique and powerful new life and position, which gives him a new scale of values. And as St. Paul said in his letter to the Ephesians 2, through Christians, God wants to show to all creation, the true riches, the riches that remain after death, the eternal riches, the riches of His grace and mercy manifested in the redemption of human beings, whose sins have been forgiven by having accepted Christ's redemptive work on the cross, confirmed by His resurrection. Therefore the apostle added: "By grace you have been saved through faith". And that salvation has not been obtained by ourselves, by our own effort or personal merit, but has been granted to us by God. Therefore, dear reader, that salvation is within your reach right now.

# 2 Kings 20:20-22:6

As we continue our study today of chapter 20 of this Second Book of Kings, let's begin our Bible reading with verses 20 and 21, to consider

## The death of Hezekiah

*"Now the rest of the acts of Hezekiah, and his exploits, and how he made the pool and the conduit to supply the city with water, are they not written in the book of the chronicles of the kings of Judah? Hezekiah slept with his fathers, and in his stead reigned his son Manasseh".*

Now, it may be unpleasant to admit that we think it would have been better if Hezekiah had died when Isaiah announced to him that the appointed time had come. Three crazy events occurred after God prolonged his life. First, he showed his treasures to Babylon, which would cause great trouble in the future. Secondly, he begot Manasseh, who would become the most wicked king of all. And lastly, in his later years, he manifested an arrogance, almost insolent. His heart was filled with pride. In the Second Book of Chronicles, chapter 32, verse 25, we read: "But Hezekiah did not return the good that was done to him, but his heart was lifted up, so that wrath came upon him, upon Judah and Jerusalem". This is why we say that perhaps it would have been better if Hezekiah had died at the time originally appointed by God.

That is why we must be very careful. The Lord has saved us and we must not do anything that will bring Him dishonor. Dear reader, this chapter 20, of the Second Book of Kings, is a great chapter. It confirms to us that we have a wonderful Heavenly Father.

And now we move on to

# 2 Kings 21

The general theme is the evil reign of Manasseh, which caused prophecies against Judah. We also have the evil reign of Amon, who was murdered by his servants, and the murderers were in turn killed by the people. Manasseh, son of Hezekiah was the most evil king of all, even surpassing Ahab and Jezebel. Now, since Manasseh was 12 years old when he began to reign, and Hezekiah reigned for 14 years, after being healed of his illness, we know then that Manasseh was born after Hezekiah's improvement. Amon succeeded Manasseh on the throne and was as bad as his father was. His servants conspired against him and put him to death in his own house. Then Josiah his son, ascended the throne of Judah.

Chapter 21 may be disappointing, after chapter 20; however it contains a great message for us. Hezekiah was the greatest king since David. There was none to compare with him. And, he was like David in other respects as well. For neither of these two men was a good father. Hezekiah fathered a son who was the worst king that ever reigned in the southern kingdom, in Judah. Indeed, it is disheartening to read about Manasseh, Hezekiah's son, seeing what he became. Now, we cannot confirm the claim we are about to make, but we believe that the "shekinah" glory, the visible presence of God, which Ezekiel saw in a vision, returned to heaven during the reign of Manasseh. Apparently, that glory was present during Hezekiah's reign, and we do not see any event after Manasseh's reign that would have caused the departure of God's visible presence. When God's presence departed from the Temple, it became a desolate place, abandoned by God. Just as our Lord said in His times, the Temple was left desolate by God. He said in the Gospel according to Matthew, chapter 23, verse 38: "Your house is left unto you desolate". As we look at the life of this man, Manasseh, we will see his hatred for the temple and for the affairs of God. Well, let us begin then by reading the first verse of this chapter 21 of the Second Book of Kings, which begins the paragraph titled

## The sins of Manasseh

> *"Twelve years old Manasseh was when he began to reign, and he reigned in Jerusalem fifty-five years. His mother's name was Hepsibah".*

Manasseh began his reign as a boy of twelve. And, as he grew older, he became more wicked. He reigned for fifty-five years, and God gave him many opportunities to change his behavior. In 2 Chronicles we find that he finally repented. God, dear reader, is always patient. God does not want anyone to perish.

We see that the name of Manasseh's mother is mentioned. Her name was Hepsiba. And she will have to accept responsibility for her son's behavior. And if there is any merit, she will be recognized. She may have been a good mother, we don't know that. We don't know how Hepsiba raised this boy, but the fact is that Manasseh was as bad as he could be. Let's read now, verse 2:

> *"But he did evil in the sight of the Lord, imitating the abominations of the nations whom the Lord had driven out from before the children of Israel".*

Manasseh was as bad as any heathen that God expelled from the land, when He brought into that territory His people. And we continue reading verse 3:

> *"He rebuilt the high places which Hezekiah his father had broken down, set up altars to Baal, and made an image of Asherah, as Ahab king of Israel had done. He worshiped also all the host of heaven and worshiped those things".*

Now, let us remember that Hezekiah had destroyed the pagan places of worship, and that a partial renovation took place under his influence. All his work was frustrated because Manasseh then re-erected those altars to Baal. He worshipped all the stars of the heavens and served them. And that means that he worshiped the sun, the moon, the stars, and all the hosts of the heavens. This worship had much in common with the later pagan worship of the Greek gods, such as Apollo and Diana, and many others.

Now, someone will say: Ah, but we live in very different times! The truth is that we do not live in very different times. We are witnessing a resurgence of astrology, and many order their lives according to the horoscope. Let us continue now, reading verses 4 and 5:

*"And he built altars in the house of the Lord, of which the Lord had said, In Jerusalem will I put my name. And he built altars for all the host of heaven in the two courts of the house of the Lord".*

Manasseh defied Almighty God. He built pagan altars in the very city of which God had said, "I will put my name here" Let us now read verse 6:

*"Moreover, he made his son to pass through the fire and was given to observing the times, he was an augur and instituted enchanters and soothsayers, thus multiplying the evil of his deeds in the sight of the Lord to provoke him to wrath".*

He even had his own son burned. This means that he resumed human sacrifice at that time. They had the custom of heating an image red-hot and then placing a small child in it as an offering. That was a horrible, sadistic and idolatrous form of satanic worship. Let us continue, now, reading verses 7 and 8 of this chapter 21 of the Second Book of Kings:

*"And he set up an image of Asherah made by him in the house of which the Lord had said to David and to Solomon his son, 'I will put my name*

*forever on this house and on Jerusalem, which I have chosen out of all the tribes of Israel. I will not again make Israel to wander far from the land which I gave to their fathers, provided they do all that I have commanded them and keep it, according to all the law which Moses my servant commanded them".*

Those people did not know it at the time, but they were about to travel. They would be taken into captivity in Babylon, because the land in which they dwelt had been theirs on one condition: obedience. Verse 9 says:

*"But they did not listen, and Manasseh led them to do worse than the nations which the Lord destroyed before the children of Israel".*

Now, not only was Manasseh as wicked as the heathen, he was worse than they were. But God would not tolerate the wickedness of the Israelites and would make them leave the land. Let's continue reading verses 10 through 13 of this 21st chapter of the Second Book of Kings:

*"Therefore thus saith the Lord by his servants the prophets, saying, Because Manasseh king of Judah hath committed these abominations, and hath done worse than all that the Amorites did before him, and hath also made Judah to sin with their idols: therefore thus saith the Lord, the God of Israel, I will bring such great evil upon Jerusalem and upon Judah, that whosoever heareth it shall have both his ears to tingle. I will measure Jerusalem with the same measure as Samaria and the same plummet as the house of Ahab. I will wipe Jerusalem as one wipes a dish that is scrubbed and turned upside down".*

Just as God had judged Samaria and all the people of Israel, God was now going to judge Jerusalem and Judah. God said that He was going to cleanse Jerusalem in the same way that a dish is cleaned. That is, God was going to perform a thorough cleansing. Jerusalem was His land, as if it were "His dish," and the Israelites had soiled it. And God was going to expel them from that land.

Dear reader, have you ever thought for a moment that you had no need of God? But you are walking on God's earth; inhaling His air, enjoying His sunshine, and drinking His water. He, as Creator, gave you the body you have. Let us, then, tell you that God says that from time to time, He washes His dishes. Nations of all centuries lie along the highway of time, and they lie in ruins. Do you know why? Because they did the same thing that many individuals and societies do today: they lived without God; they thought they didn't need God. Dear reader, God said that He was going to clean Jerusalem as one cleans a dish. And let's continue reading verse 14 of this chapter 21 of the Second Book of Kings:

> *"I will abandon the rest of my inheritance and give it into the hands of their enemies; they shall be a prey and a spoil to all their adversaries".*

God said that he would cease to hold back the waters of the dam, and the enemy would then come in like a flood. Let us now continue to consider Manasseh. Let us read verse 16:

> *"Moreover, Manasseh shed such innocent blood that he filled Jerusalem from end to end, apart from the sin wherewith he made Judah to sin, that he might do evil in the sight of the Lord".*

When a man or a nation sins, it sins not in one way, but in many ways. And many societies have forgotten God, to such an extent that immorality is being accepted as something normal, or as an option that can be freely chosen. And there are still people who are surprised that aggressiveness is increasing among the youngest, not only in the street but even in schools! Well, we cannot flee from physical and psychological violence until we take the first and decisive step of returning to God. That is the first step. And we continue reading verses 17 and 18:

> "The rest of the acts of Manasseh, all that he did, and the sin that he committed, are they not written in the book of the chronicles of the kings of Judah? Manasseh slept with his fathers and was buried in the garden of his own house, in the garden of Uzzah. And Amon his son reigned in his stead.

This, then, is the story of Manasseh. There is not much more to say about him, except that he was depraved, corrupt, and that at last he died. Let us now read verses 19 to 22 of this chapter 21 of the Second Book of Kings, to consider

## The brief reign of Amon

> "Twenty-two years old was Amon when he began to reign, and he reigned two years in Jerusalem. His mother's name was Meshuremos, the daughter of Haruz of Jothbah. And he did evil in the sight of the Lord, as Manasseh his father had done. He walked in all the ways in which his father walked, and served the idols which his father had served, and worshiped them. He forsook the Lord, the God of his fathers, and walked not in the way of the Lord".

Amon followed the bad example of his father. He abandoned the Lord. Consequently, the Lord also abandoned him. Verse 23 says:

> "The servants of Amon conspired against him and killed the king in his house".

Amon's wickedness led to a revolution. At times it seems that the conflicts in society are becoming greater and greater, which is also reflected at the international level. Dear reader, truly, we live in dangerous times. Now, this section leads us to the last of the great kings. One of the greatest renewal movements occurred during his reign.

## 2 Kings 22:1-6

The general theme of chapters 22 and 23 is the good reign of Josiah, who began to reign when he was 8 years old and reigned for 31 years. He was one of the best kings who reigned after Solomon. During his reign, the nation experienced a great and necessary spiritual renewal. Hilkiah, the high priest, was his counselor and assistant. Let us read, then, verses 1 and 2, which begin the account of

## The good reign of Josiah in Judah

*"When Josiah began to reign he was eight years old, and he reigned in Jerusalem thirty-one years. His mother's name was Jedidah, the daughter of Adaiah of Boschath. He did that which was right in the sight of the Lord, and walked in all the way of David his father, and turned not aside to the right hand or to the left".*

It was like watching the sun rising in a new dawn. And the light shone once again in that land. Josiah had come to the throne and would lead the most important renewal that the people had had since the times of David and Solomon.

It should be considered that a renewal begins as an individual, personal experience and not with the spectacular nature of a mass movement. In this case, it began with the man at the highest level of government. And his deeds were right in the eyes of the Lord. We have then, the steps of that renovation which were as follows: first, the Temple was repaired. Secondly, there was a new discovery of the Word of God. Thirdly, the people were convinced of their sin. Fourthly, an eradication of idolatry. Fifth, there was also a repudiation of immorality. Sixth, the celebration of the Passover was reinstated. And seventhly, there was a reformation.

Now, recalling some background and historical context, we will say that Josiah was king over the southern kingdom of Judah. You will recall that the northern kingdom had already been taken into captivity during the reign of Hezekiah in the south, who was another benign and outstanding king. Then Manasseh and Amon, both wicked kings, came to the throne of Judah. And now, Josiah was on the throne. During his reign, the prophets Nahum, Habakkuk, Zephaniah and Jeremiah acted.

Let's continue now with chapter 22 of the Second Book of Kings and read verses 3 and 4, which tell us about

## The repair of the temple

> *"In the eighteenth year of King Josiah the king sent Shaphan the son of Azaliah the son of Meshullam, the scribe, to the house of the Lord, saying, 'Go to the high priest Hilkiah and tell him to collect the money that has been brought into the house of the Lord and has been collected from the people by the keepers of the gate.'"*

The first thing he did was to act righteously before the Lord, and the second thing he did was to repair the temple. Now, apparently the Temple was not in use when Josiah came to the throne. It had become a kind of storehouse, a repository of leftovers and refuse. Let's continue reading verses 5 and 6:

> *"Let it be put into the hands of those who do the work, those who have charge of the repair of the house of the Lord, that they may give it to those who do the work of the house of the Lord, to those who repair the cracks in the House, to the carpenters, masters and masons, and wood and hewn stone may be purchased to repair the House".*

Here we see that the king told the people to take care of repairing the temple.

Christianity in general today is very similar to the Temple of Josiah's time. It is in great need of repair, that is, of a great renovation. We are not talking about the buildings. For there are many beautiful buildings that serve as Temples. We are talking about a return to the Word of God which, by itself, cleanses, purifies, and with the action of the Holy Spirit, removes everything that hinders the relationship of the body of believers with their Lord. We refer to the presence of ideas foreign to the Word of God that have accumulated in its interior, or to cracks of spiritual character, which threaten the unity and stability of many believers who compose the church. These factors impede its growth and full fulfillment of its work, which is the great mission of testimony that the Lord entrusted to his disciples when he commissioned them to go into all the world preaching the Gospel to all.

But previously, when considering that this reformation began by King Josiah himself, we said that all reformation, all renewal begins on a personal, individual level, when a person establishes a relationship with God through the Lord Jesus Christ, or when a person who is already a believer is aware of elements in his life or character that constitute an impediment to a full relationship with the Lord. Dear reader, you yourself, more than anyone else, know where and how you stand before God.

# 2 Kings 22:8-23:25

W e continue studying today, chapter 22 of the Second Book of Kings. And in the previous chapter, we were talking about king Josiah, of Judah, in the south. And we said that he had led the greatest renewal movement that this people had ever experienced, after the days of David and Solomon. The northern kingdom had already been taken into captivity during the reign of Hezekiah in the south, who was another extraordinary king. After Hezekiah, his son Manasseh reigned, and after him, Amon, both wicked kings, who reigned in Judah.

But now, Josiah was on the throne. And we saw that he reigned for 31 years and was a good king. During his reign, Nahum, Habakkuk, Zephaniah and Jeremiah, were the prophets. We saw later, that the first thing Josiah did, was to act righteously in the sight of the Lord. The second thing Josiah did, was to have the Temple repaired. The Temple was apparently not in use when Josiah ascended the throne. It had become a kind of storehouse, a repository for leftovers and refuse. But Josiah commanded the people to work and to get busy repairing the Temple. And we said that the church, today, is very similar to the Temple of Josiah's time, because it needs certain repairs.

We are not talking about the buildings. There are many beautiful buildings that serve as temples. Christianity in general today is very much like the Temple of Josiah's time. It is in great need of repair, that is, of a great renovation. We are not talking about the buildings. For there are many beautiful buildings that serve as Temples. We are talking about a return to the Word of God which, by itself, cleanses, purifies, and with the action of the Holy Spirit, removes everything that hinders the relationship of the body of believers with their Lord. We refer to the presence of ideas foreign to the Word of God that have accumulated in its interior, or to cracks of spiritual character, which threaten the unity and stability of many believers who compose the church. These factors impede its growth and full fulfillment of its work, which is the great mission of testimony that the Lord entrusted to his disciples when he charged them to go into all the world preaching the Gospel to all. This reform began by King Josiah himself, we said that all reform, all renewal begins at a personal, individual level.

This king Josiah put an end to all the idolatry that was in the city of Jerusalem. The idols that had been set up by his grandfather Manasseh, were removed. Let us read verse 8 of this chapter 22 of this Second Book of Kings, where we see that

## The book of the law was discovered

*Then Hilkiah the high priest said to Shaphan the scribe, "I have found the book of the Law in the house of the LORD. And Hilkiah delivered the book to Shaphan, who read it".*

The third thing they did that brought a renewal to the nation was a return to the Word of God. They had lost the Bible, and they had lost it in the temple. But they found that Word and made it the standard of their lives. The Word of God is the only thing we have as a weapon. It is the Word of God that has life and power and is sharper than any two-edged sword (Hebrews 4:12). There is no shortcut, no convenient route, no new method for renewal.

Do you remember the case of Joseph and Mary, the parents of Jesus? When Jesus was a child his earthly parents lost him in the Temple. We should be vigilant to prevent both Jesus and the Bible from being lost in the church of our time. At that time, Hilkiah the high priest found the Word of God in the Temple. It had been lost inside the Temple. And the Bible, Dear Reader, has to be the beginning of a renewal.

Let us continue reading now, and read verses 9 and 10 of this chapter 22 of the Second Book of Kings:

> *"Then Shaphan the scribe stood before the king and reported to him, saying, 'Your servants have collected the money that was found in the Temple and have given it to those who are doing the work, those who are in charge of repairing the house of the Lord. And Shaphan the scribe said to the king, "Hilkiah the priest has given me a book. Shaphan read it before the king.*

Let's imagine the scene. King Josiah was listening for the first time to the reading of the Word of God. Let us read here verse 11:

> *"When the king heard the words of the book of the Law, he rent his clothes".*

The fourth step toward renewal is repentance. The reading of God's Word brought repentance. When the king heard the Word of God, he tore his clothes, as a sign of deep emotion. Why? Because the Word of God brought conviction and revealed their sin and brought Without the Word of God they were unaware of how far they had strayed from God's Law. A return to God's Word brings renewal. Let us now read verse 13:

> *"Go and inquire of the Lord for me, for the people and for all Judah, concerning the words of this book which has been found, for great is the anger of the Lord which is kindled against us, because our fathers did not listen to the words of this book and have not acted according to all that is written in it".*

The king was frightened to realize that they deserved God's judgment. The message with which God responded to Josiah through Huldah, the prophetess, revealed both God's justice and grace. Let us read verses 16 and 17 of this chapter 22 of the Second Book of Kings:

> "Thus saith the Lord, I will bring upon this place, and upon the inhabitants thereof, all the evil spoken of in this book which the king of Judah hath read, because they have forsaken me, and burned incense unto other gods, provoking me to anger with all the work of their hands. My wrath is kindled against this place, and it shall not be quenched".

But now let us observe God's grace towards King Josiah. Let us read verses 19 and 20:

> "and your heart was tender and you have humbled yourself before the Lord in hearing what I have spoken against this place and against its inhabitants, that they shall be desolate and cursed, and because you have torn your clothes and wept before me, I also have heard you, says the Lord. Therefore I will cause thee to be gathered to thy fathers: thou shalt be brought to thy grave in peace, and thine eyes shall see none of the evils which I bring upon this place".

And they brought the answer to the king.

We have here, the prophecy against the kingdom of Judah and all the evil that God would bring as judgment on Judah. But we see that God promises Josiah that he would die in peace and that he would not see all this judgment that would come upon Judah. And the reason for God to deliver Josiah, we find it here in the last part of verse 18 and the first part of verse 19. It says, "Because thou hast heard the words of the book, and thine heart was tender, and thou hast humbled thyself before the Lord". And, Dear reader, for there to be a true renewal in Christianity today, we need to hear the Words of the Book very carefully; we need to turn to the Word of God. And secondly, we need to humble ourselves before God.

And so we arrive at

## 2 Kings 23:1-25

And in this chapter the following events stand out: Josiah had the book read in a solemn assembly. He renewed the covenant of the Lord. He destroyed idolatry and all its aftermath. He burned the bones of the dead on the altar of Bethel, as foretold. He celebrated a very solemn Passover. Then the final wrath of God was manifested against Judah. Josiah died at Megiddo. He was succeeded on the throne by the evil kings Jehoahaz and later Jehoiakim. Let us read verses 1 to 3, which initiate the paragraph of

## Josiah's additional reforms

*"Then the king commanded to summon before him all the elders of Judah and Jerusalem. Then the king went up to the house of the Lord with all the men of Judah and all the inhabitants of Jerusalem, the priests, the prophets, and all the people, from the least to the greatest. There he read aloud all the words of the book of the covenant that had been found in the house of the Lord. Then, standing at the pillar, the king made a covenant before the Lord, pledging that they would follow the Lord and keep his commandments, his testimonies, and his statutes, with all their heart and with all their soul, and that they would keep the words of the covenant that were written in that book. And all the people confirmed the covenant".*

We see that the people said that they would not only read the Word of God, but also put it into practice, living according to its standards. We have already said that for renewal to take place there must be a conviction of sin, which only the Word of God can bring. When the Bible brings that conviction to the heart, repentance must follow. Repentance consists of turning around and heading in the opposite direction. If one is going the wrong way, he turns around to change direction.

Josiah as king had tremendous influence. He put into operation a very bold plan. He began by removing idolatry from the temple of God. It says here in this 23rd chapter of the Second Book of Kings, verse 4:

> *"The king commanded Hilkiah the high priest, the priests of the second order, and the gatekeepers, to bring out of the temple of the Lord all the vessels that had been made for Baal, Asherah, and all the host of heaven. He burned them outside Jerusalem, in the field of Kidron, and had their ashes brought to Bethel".*

All things that had to do with the worship of false gods were burned in the fields of Kidron, outside Jerusalem. The ashes were then taken out of town, so that the people could not even see them. So, Josiah banished immorality. Let us continue now, reading verse 7:

> *"Moreover he tore down the places of idolatrous prostitution that were in the house of the Lord, in which the women wove tents for Asherah".*

Josiah also interrupted the offering of human sacrifices, which consisted of sacrificing children as a sacrifice to Moloch. Let us read verse 10:

> *"He also defiled the burning place which is in the valley of the son of Hinnom, so that no man should pass his son or his daughter through fire before Molech".*

Josiah also tore down images, sculptures, statues, altars and high places that kings before him had brought into the land. He even went beyond the boundaries of Judah, going as far as Bethel. In 2 Chronicles 34:33, his activity is summarized. It says: "Josiah removed all the abominations from all the land of the children of Israel, and made all who were in Israel serve the Lord their God. And as long as he lived they did not depart from the Lord, the God of their fathers".

It was interesting that at Bethel, he saw the tomb of the prophet who had foretold that he would do all these things (1 Kings 13:2), as we can see now, as we read verses 17 and 18:

> *Then he said, "What is this monument that I see? The men of the city said to him, This is the sepulcher of the man of God who came from Judah and prophesied these things that you have done on the altar of Bethel. And the king said, Let him alone; let no man move his bones. Thus were his bones preserved, and the bones of the prophet who had come from Samaria".*

Now, let us read verses 21 to 23, where we see another important and positive step that Josiah took:

## Easter was restored

> *"Then the king commanded all the people, 'Keep the Passover to the LORD your God, according to what is written in the book of this covenant. No such Passover had been kept since the time of the judges who ruled Israel, nor in all the times of the kings of Israel and the kings of Judah. In the eighteenth year of King Josiah that Passover was kept to the Lord in Jerusalem.*

The Passover celebration constituted a great event. Apparently they had not celebrated it for a long time; they had overlooked it. Now, what did the Passover mean? The Passover was a symbol of Christ. But, the people had forgotten about it. In the New Testament the apostle Paul said, in 1 Corinthians 5:7, that Christ, who is our Passover Lamb, was slain in sacrifice for us. Today many try to have a religion, but without Christ. The deity of Christ is ridiculed even among some professing Christians. The value of Christ's death is rejected and despised, as well as the efficacy of Christ's blood. But, Dear Reader, the only thing that can revitalize Christianity is genuine renewal.

The tide of a great blessing came in the 16th century and was driven by reformers such as Martin Luther, John Calvin and Zwingli. Wyclif and John Knox had been reformers in the 14th and 15th centuries, even before the Reformation. In the 17th century there was another spiritual awakening known as the Puritan Movement. The 18th century, in a time of darkness and deism, another great spiritual awakening began, led by Wesley and Whitfield. In the 19th century there was an influential return to God in Oxford, which resulted in the Missionary Movement. Towards the end of that century great renewal movements were led by Moody and Finney. In the 20th century there has been no worldwide renewal. It is true that there have been some renewals of local character, just as others have taken place in the 21st century. We could say that, in general, we live in times of spiritual coldness and indifference. In some regions of the world, especially in those where the standard of living is more or less high, there is even a clear regression of Christianity. People's minds are captivated by other forms of idolatry, typical of the consumer society. Thoughts revolve, rather, around achieving a life of quality from the material point of view, and those who already enjoy this level, struggle to preserve and increase it in a race that seems to have no end. It is like a craving that cannot be satiated, that is never satisfied. And the new leisure and free time options, to which people cling, when they lose their novelty, are soon replaced by others. From a human realism point of view, therefore, no change in this situation is to be expected. And these tremendous forces operating at the social level seem to have cornered the Bible, the great absentee of the media, limiting its influence to certain reduced environments. But, from God's point of view, human affairs and tendencies are seen differently. Going back to the time we are studying, we saw that idolatry had invaded, had saturated all levels and institutions of society. And it is necessary to remember that what happened in the times of Josiah, when the people had gone as far as possible in their estrangement from God, should stimulate us when considering the possibilities of a renewal today. For in the darkest hour of that kingdom of Judah, a profound renewal took place in every order.

Have we ever confessed our coldness and indifference to God? Have we ever felt this conviction when we came into contact with the Word of God? Recalling the feelings of King Josiah towards the Word of God, have we felt before Him that love, that respect for what He has revealed to us in the Bible, and that desire to bring the divine Word into our practical life? Truly, we need the Word of God to penetrate every corner of our lives so that, by the power of the Holy Spirit, a true transformation may take place within us.

The prophet Isaiah, who prophesied earlier in this kingdom of Judah, in his book, 6:7, told us what he experienced before a vision of God's presence. He saw himself as he was and felt impure, unworthy to have beheld the King of kings and he expressed it. His contemporaries needed to feel the same way, given the situation of spiritual prostration in which they found themselves. Then, in the same vision, an angel from God came to him with tongs holding an ember that he had taken from the altar, and touching his mouth with it, he communicated to him the following message, which he and his people needed to hear: "Look, this ember has touched your lips. Your wickedness has been taken away, your guilt has been laid upon you". The people needed the action of God's purifying fire. And, dear reader, do we not need it ourselves?

# 2 Kings 23:26-25:30

---

We continue our study of chapter 23 of the Second Book of Kings, considering the death of Josiah. And we enter a sad part in the history of Josiah. The great renewal took place at the end of his reign. Soon his people would go into captivity. In the last days of Josiah's reign, God acted in a mighty way to reveal the fact that He can bring about a great renewal movement, even in the most difficult and darkest days. Now, what caused the end of that reformation? Let's read verse 29 of this 23rd chapter of 2 Kings:

> *"In those days Pharaoh Necho, king of Egypt, went up to the river Euphrates to meet the king of Assyria. King Josiah went out against him; but when he saw him, he slew him at Megiddo."*

Now, Pharaoh Necho went on an expedition to help the king of Assyria fight against Nabopolassar, king of Babylon. Josiah and his forces went into that fight, which was not their place to do. And this action resulted in disaster. Now, Josiah should have stayed at home. This fight did not concern Josiah, but he went out anyway, and what happened to him? He was killed at Megiddo. Josiah was a great man of God, but here he acted in a foolish way. He entered a battle that was not his to enter, and this resulted in his death. Let us continue now, reading verse 30

> *"His servants put him in a chariot, brought him dead from Megiddo to Jerusalem, and buried him in his tomb. Then the people of the land took Jehoahaz son of Josiah, anointed him and proclaimed him king in his father's place".*

Let us now read verses 31 to 33, which begin to relate that

## Jehoahaz reigned and was dethroned

*"Jehoahaz was twenty-three years old when he began to reign and reigned three months in Jerusalem. His mother's name was Hamutal, the daughter of Jeremiah of Libnah. And he did evil in the sight of the Lord, according to all that his fathers had done. Pharaoh Necho held him prisoner in Riblah, in the province of Hamath, so that he would not reign in Jerusalem, and he imposed on the country a tribute of three thousand three hundred pounds of silver and thirty-three pounds of gold".*

It was to be expected that Jehoahaz would follow the righteous conduct of his father, but he did not. He was a wicked king. The fact is that he remained on the throne for only a space of three months. Pharaoh was not pleased with his manner of ruling; so he removed him from the throne and led him into the country of Egypt, where he died. Let us continue, then, with verses 34 and 37, which inform us that

## Jehoiakim was appointed king

*"Then Pharaoh Necho made Eliakim the son of Josiah king instead of Josiah his father, and changed his name to Jehoiakim. He took Jehoahaz and carried him away to Egypt, where he died. But he did evil in the sight of the Lord, according to all that his fathers had done".*

Jehoiakim was another son of Josiah and reigned for 11 years, but he was also a bad king. The affairs of the kingdom went from bad to worse. Jehoahaz was evil, but Jehoiakim was even worse. If Jehoahaz had been bad, Jehoiakim was even worse.

At that time, Babylon, a great power, was rising in the east, on the Euphrates River. Babylon was displacing Assyria. The fact was that Babylon defeated Assyria. Babylon would also defeat Egypt and thus become the first great world power, as we will see as we study the book of Daniel. And it is at this time that we should read the book of Jeremiah, because Jeremiah was the great prophet who lived during this time. And it was he who called the inhabitants of Judah warning them that if they did not turn to God, they would be taken captive to Babylon. But, Jeremiah's words seemed incredible to the inhabitants of Judah, because in those times Nebuchadnezzar, king of Babylon, was not yet considered a formidable enemy. On the other hand, the false prophets told the nation that God could not spare them and would never destroy them as a nation. Jerusalem was God's city; His holy temple was there and they were His chosen people. In reality, He did not need the temple, which would soon be destroyed. And the Temple was destroyed.

## 2 Kings 24

The general theme of chapters 24 and 25 presents us with the kingdom of Judah being led into captivity. Turning now to chapter 24 of this Second Book of Kings, we have the following events: Nebuchadnezzar king of Babylon, attacked Jehoiakim and Judah was defeated. This was God's judgment on the nation, due to the sins of Manasseh. After the death of Jehoiakim, who had reigned for 11 years, his son Jehoiakim, came to the throne where he remained for only 3 months. He was also a bad king. The king of Babylon took Jerusalem, sacked it and took captive all the nobles, among whom were Daniel and the 3 Hebrew youths. Nebuchadnezzar also took captive King Jehoiakim to Babylon and placed in his place as king his uncle Mattaniah, and changed his name to Zedekiah. Zedekiah was also a bad king and rebelled against Nebuchadnezzar. Let us begin, then, with this chapter 24, reading the first verse, in which we see that

## Nebuchadnezzar came against Judah

*"In his time Nebuchadnezzar king of Babylon came up on campaign, and Jehoiakim became his servant for three years, but then he again rebelled against him".*

Pharaoh of Egypt had placed Jehoiakim on the throne, but he lost all his Asian possessions to Nebuchadnezzar of Babylon. Now when Nebuchadnezzar came against Judah, Jehoiakim submitted for three years and then rebelled against him. Let's read verses 2 and 3:

*"The Lord sent against Jehoiakim forces of Chaldeans, Syrians, Moabites, and Ammonites. He sent them against Judah to destroy it, according to the word which the Lord had spoken by his servants the prophets. Surely this came against Judah at the commandment of the Lord, to remove her from his presence, because of all the sins committed by Manasseh".*

We have already said that Manasseh had been a wicked man. If the glory of the Lord did not depart from the temple during his reign, nothing worse that happened afterwards could have caused it to depart. Because the children of Israel did not turn away from the sins of Manasseh, they would have to be taken into captivity. Verse 4 says:

*"for all the sins committed by Manasseh and also for the innocent blood that he shed, for he filled Jerusalem with innocent blood. Therefore the Lord would not forgive".*

While it is true that God forgives all sin, the sinner must come to Him in repentance. Dear reader, He is the only one in the world who can forgive your sin. He died for you and paid the penalty, the punishment for your sins. Who else could forgive your sins? He alone is the way, the truth and the life. Let us read verses 5 through 7 of this chapter 24 of the Second Book of Kings, where we see that

## Jehoiakim died and was succeeded by Jehoiachin on the

throne.

*"The rest of the acts of Jehoiakim, and all that he did, are they not written in the book of the chronicles of the kings of Judah? Jehoiakim slept with his fathers, and Jehoiakim his son reigned in his stead. The king of Egypt never went out of his land again, for the king of Babylon took all that was his from the river of Egypt to the river Euphrates".*

These are the exact boundaries of the land that God had granted to Abraham. But here we see that Babylon controlled that whole area, instead of Israel. Let us continue reading verses 8 and 9:

*"Jehoiachin was eighteen years old when he began to reign and reigned in Jerusalem three months. His mother's name was Nehusta, daughter of Elnathan of Jerusalem. And he did evil in the sight of the Lord, according to all that his father had done".*

Well, the reason they lost that land was because Israel had continued in their sin and rebellion against God. Let us remember that God had granted them possession of the land on one condition, which was their obedience. Although the land was theirs by an unconditional covenant, the occupation was conditional and they failed to fulfill that condition. Let us go a little further, reading verses 10 through 12, which begin the story in which

## Jehoiachin was taken captive (first deportation)

*"At that time the servants of Nebuchadnezzar king of Babylon came up against Jerusalem, and the city was besieged. Nebuchadnezzar king of Babylon also came to the city, while his servants besieged it. Then Jehoiakim king of Judah, along with his mother, his servants, his princes, and his officers, surrendered to the king of Babylon. In the eighth year of his reign the king of Babylon took him prisoner".*

The king and all the nobles were then taken in the first group that went into captivity. This occurred around 605 B.C. Let's move on, reading verses 13 through 15:

> "Then he brought out from there all the treasures of the house of the Lord and the treasures of the royal house. As the Lord had said, he broke in pieces all the vessels of gold that Solomon king of Israel had made in the house of the Lord. He took captive all Jerusalem, all the princes and all the mighty men of valor, ten thousand captives, and all the craftsmen and smiths; none were left except the poor people of the land. Also Jehoiachin, and the king's mother, and the king's wives, and his officers, and the mighty men of the land, were carried away captive from Jerusalem to Babylon".

As you see, Dear Reader, this is a sad and sordid story. Let us now read verses 17 to 19, in which we see that

## Zedekiah was made king by Nebuchadnezzar

> "Then the king of Babylon made Mattaniah, his uncle, king in Jehoiachin's place, and changed his name to Zedekiah. Zedekiah was twenty-one years old when he began to reign and reigned in Jerusalem eleven years. His mother's name was Hamutal, daughter of Jeremiah of Libnah. He did evil in the sight of the Lord, according to all that Jehoiakim had done".

Zedekiah was Jehoiachin's uncle. Now, he did not improve the line of kings in any way. It was to be hoped that captivity would make him sensible, but, it did not. Hardship does one of two things for the individual: It either makes him tender; or it hardens him. Either they bring him closer to God, or they drive him away from Him. It is never possible for one to be the same after experiencing affliction and suffering. The same sun that melts the wax, hardens the clay. Let us now read verse 20 of this chapter 24 of the Second Book of Kings:

*"So the anger of the Lord came against Jerusalem and Judah, until he drove them out of his presence. Then Zedekiah rebelled against the king of Babylon".*

Again, the false prophets said, "Look, God is with us". But God was not with Israel at this time, because Israel was not with God. Dear reader, we must be extremely careful of presumption and boldness when we claim that something we do is God's Will, and that He has not revealed that Will to us. And they go ahead doing what they themselves want to do. And then, it turns out that they fail, and that it was not God's Will. Recall that the false prophets in Israel claimed that God was with them. And it turns out that God had nothing to do with them. Instead of making sure that God is on our side, we should make sure that we are on His side.

This was the problem of the people of Judah. They were far from God, and yet they thought that because they were God's people, He would protect them.

## 2 Kings 25

In this chapter we have the final deportation of Judah. Nebuchadnezzar, king of Babylon, came 3 times to Jerusalem. He deported the royalty, the military and the skilled workers. But he did not destroy the city until he came to it the third time. Zedekiah's eyes were gouged out after he saw his own sons slain. Nebuchadnezzar also burned the Temple and transported everything of value to Babylon, including all the Temple utensils. Jerusalem was then totally destroyed. Nebuchadnezzar appointed Gedaliah as governor, who became the servile subject of King Nebuchadnezzar. And before long, he was killed and those who were left still fled to Egypt. Also in this chapter, Jehoiachin was released from prison in Babylon and there received a position of prominence. We have seen that Nebuchadnezzar had appointed Zedekiah as king of Judah, but after a few years, Zedekiah rebelled and now we will see that Nebuchadnezzar came for the last time and ended the kingdom of Judah for good. Let's read the first 2 verses of this chapter 25 of the Second Book of Kings, where the story begins of

## The fall of Jerusalem

> *"And it came to pass in the ninth year of his reign, in the tenth day of the tenth month, that Nebuchadnezzar king of Babylon came with all his army against Jerusalem, and besieged it, and set up towers round about it. The city was besieged until the eleventh year of king Zedekiah".*

The accuracy of the date indicates the great importance of this site, which was the beginning of the end for Jerusalem. Verse 3 says:

> *"On the ninth day of the fourth month the famine raged in the city, and when the people of the land had no more to eat".*

The intensity of the suffering of the people is described in the book of Lamentations. Let us continue reading verses 4 to 6:

> *"Then they broke through the wall of the city. Although the Chaldeans had it surrounded, all the men of war fled during the night by the way of the gate that was between the two walls, by the king's gardens. The king went by the way of the Arabah, but the army of the Chaldeans pursued him and seized him in the plains of Jericho, having scattered all his army. So they took the king prisoner and brought him to Riblah before the king of Babylon, and passed sentence on him.*

Here we see that the enemy broke into the city, and then the king and his troops tried to escape. But they were captured. The prophet Jeremiah had predicted the fall of Jerusalem and was considered a traitor because he told the people the truth. Verse 7 says:

*"They slew Zedekiah's sons before him, and put out his eyes, and bound him with chains, and carried him to Babylon".*

This man was deceived by the false prophets, but would not listen to God's prophet. So he was taken into captivity, but blind. Let us now read verse 9, which tells us

## The fire in Jerusalem

*"He set on fire the house of the Lord, the house of the king, and all the houses of Jerusalem; he also set on fire all the houses of the princes".*

Because of Jerusalem's rebellion, Nebuchadnezzar burned and razed the city to the ground in such a way that when the prophet Nehemiah entered the city seventy years after the captivity and saw the place, it seemed almost impossible to rebuild. But, he revived the people by recognizing that the most important problem he had to overcome was discouragement. Nebuchadnezzar's armies, therefore, devastated the city. The false prophets had insisted that God would not allow the people to be taken captive, nor the city to be destroyed.

Let us continue now, reading verses 10 through 12:

*"All the army of the Chaldeans that accompanied the captain of the guard broke down the walls that surrounded Jerusalem. Then Nebuzaradan, the captain of the guard, took captive those of the people who were left in the city, those who had gone over to the king of Babylon, and those who were left of the common people. Nebuzaradan, captain of the guard, left some of the poor of the land to till the vineyards and the land".*

Here we see that they left those who were of no value to them. They also wanted the land to continue to produce, so that they could exact tribute from them. Let us continue reading verses 13 and 14:

> *"The Chaldeans broke the bronze pillars that were in the house of the Lord, the pillars and the huge bronze basin for water that was in the house of the Lord, and carried the bronze away to Babylon. Also the Chaldeans took away the ashtrays, the shovels, the tongs, the ladles, and all the bronze utensils for worship".*

Nebuchadnezzar's army practically emptied the Temple before destroying it with fire. All the wealth they found, they took it to Babylon. And when we come to the Book of Daniel, we will have occasion to find that those temple utensils were put away and brought out when King Belshazzar held his great banquet. Here we see that Jerusalem was sacked, burned and turned into a heap of rubble.

Jerusalem has been destroyed some twenty-seven times. And each time the city has been rebuilt over the previous ruins. The hill on which Jerusalem stands today is a city that has largely been built on the ruins of past cities. Turning then to verse 24, let us see that

## Gedaliah was appointed governor

> *"Gedaliah swore an oath to them and theirs, and said to them, "Do not be afraid to serve the Chaldeans; dwell in the land, serve the king of Babylon, and it will be well with you.*

He was appointed to rule the people who were left in the land. They should have listened to the prophet Jeremiah, who begged them to settle there and accept this form of government. Instead, they murdered the governor Gedaliah. And verses 25 and 26 say:

> *"But in the seventh month came Ishmael the son of Nethaniah the son of Elishama, of the royal seed, accompanied by ten men, and they smote and killed Gedaliah, and those of Judah and the Chaldeans who were with him at Mizpah. Then all the people arose, from the least to the greatest,*

*with the captains of the army, and went to Egypt for fear of the Chaldeans".*

A large group fled to Egypt, becoming settlers there. By the way, Jeremiah went with this group, although not willingly, for he was forced. Finally, let us read verses 27 to 30, where we see that

## Joaquín was released

*"Now it came to pass in the thirty-seventh year of the captivity of Jehoiakim king of Judah, in the twelfth month, on the twenty-seventh day of the month, that Evil-merodach king of Babylon, in the first year of his reign, released Jehoiakim king of Judah, bringing him out of prison. He spoke kindly to him and set his throne higher than the thrones of the kings who were with him in Babylon. He changed his prisoner's garments, and Jehoiachin always ate before him all the days of his life. His food was given him daily from the king, day after day, all the days of his life".*

Evil-merodach enacted an amnesty upon his accession to the throne of Babylon. Although there were other kings captured at his court, Jehoiachin was given a position of honor among them. Interestingly, the period of the kings concludes with the kindness with which this last descendant of King David, who had grown old in a Babylonian prison, was treated.

And so, Dear Reader, we conclude our study of this chapter 25, and with it, our study of the Second Book of Kings. God willing, in our next chapter, we will leave the Old Testament and turn to the New Testament to begin our study of the Apostle Paul's letter to the Romans. The book ends with the execution of God's righteous judgment, after giving His people the greatest opportunities to repent and rectify. And since He, before the time comes for Him to be judge, must be a God who saves, he says: (2 Corinthians 6:2) "Behold, now is the proper time: behold, now is the day of salvation".

# Conclusion

The book of 2 Kings offers us a profound reflection on the history of Israel and Judah, emphasizing the importance of faithfulness to God. Through the stories of kings and prophets, we are taught that the decisions of the leaders have a significant impact on the people. Disobedience and idolatry lead to destruction, while loyalty and the pursuit of righteousness bring blessings.

One of the most valuable lessons is the need to heed and follow the warnings of the prophets. Often ignored, these divine messengers remind us that wisdom and spiritual guidance are essential for a fulfilled life. The story of the kings shows us that repentance and restoration are always possible, giving us hope in times of crisis.

**1.** Although Satan tries to destroy God's plans, he will never succeed (11:1-3). Athaliah tried to destroy the king's offspring.

**2.** When nations turn away from God, sooner or later there will be consequences (Gal. 6:7). This was the case with all the nations that strayed in ancient times: every one of them suffered the consequences of forsaking God.

It is not good to be silent about the good news of salvation (7:9; Rom 1:14-15). "We are not doing right" - We must preach the gospel of Christ or our wickedness will catch up with us.

**4.** When God is with us, even though we are few, we become more (6:16, 17; Rom 8:31; Heb 13:5).

**5.** Doing good to enemies brings good results (6:21-23; Rom 12:20; Matt 5:44).

**6.** Obedience brings excellent results (5:1-15).

**7.** Like father, like son (15:34) Jotham did all that his father Uzziah had done.

**8.** God does not accept or take pleasure in the commandments of men (17:19-20; Matthew 15:7-9).

**9.** Men can make idols of many things (18:4). That is why today we do not have many things that many can worship (the writings of Jesus, the body of Moses, etc.).

**10.** One angel can kill 185,000 men. Now imagine if there were more than 12 legions of angels (Matthew 26:53).

**11.** Mocking others can have serious consequences (2:23-24).

# Don't miss out!

Visit the website below and you can sign up to receive emails whenever Bible Sermons publishes a new book. There's no charge and no obligation.

https://books2read.com/r/B-A-MZBS-YMAJF

**BOOKS2READ**

Connecting independent readers to independent writers.

Did you love *Bible Class for Adults and Youth: Beginner's Guide: 2 Kings*? Then you should read *Bible Class for Youth and Adults: Beginner's Guide: The Pentateuch*[1] by Bible Sermons!

[2]

**Bible study series chapter by chapter, ideal for young people and adults.**

In general terms, it can be stated that the Pentateuch begins with the creation of the universe and concludes with the death of Moses. Through these books, the history of Israel, the people chosen by God according to various religious doctrines, is narrated.

The Pentateuch is considered essential to understand the Bible as a whole. According to believers, it contains divine revelation to the chosen people and reflections on God's purpose for humanity.

---

1. https://books2read.com/u/3GJXka

2. https://books2read.com/u/3GJXka

Historically, the Pentateuch is significant because it recounts the history of humanity, even though it focuses on God's chosen people. It is important to remember that the biblical texts possess a breadth and depth that allow their teachings to apply to our lives, regardless of time and place; *they are stories that transcend time and space barriers, with great teachings and applications for life.*

# Also by Bible Sermons

**A Collection of Biblical Sermons**
The Power of Great Gospel Words
The Power of Prayer: Men Ought Always to Pray
The Power of the Single Life in Christ
Analyzing The Power of a Life in Christ

**Bible Characters Collection**
Analyzing Biblical Scenes: 62 Inspiring Christian Teachings from the Old Testament

**BIBLE CLASS FROM SCRATCH**
Bible Class for Youth and Adults: Beginner's Guide: Genesis
Bible Class for Youth and Adults: Beginner's Guide: Exodus
Bible Class for Youth and Adults: Beginner's Guide: Leviticus
Bible Class for Youth and Adults: Beginner's Guide: Numbers
Bible Class for Youth and Adults: Beginner's Guide: Deuteronomy
Bible Class for Adults and Youth: Beginner's Guide: Joshua
Bible Class for Adults and Youth: Beginner's Guide: Judges
Bible Class for Adults and Youth: Beginner's Guide: Ruth
Bible Class for Adults and Youth: Beginner's Guide: 1 Samuel

Bible Class for Adults and Youth: Beginner's Guide: 2 Samuel
Bible Class for Adults and Youth: Beginner's Guide: 1 Kings
Bible Class for Adults and Youth: Beginner's Guide: 2 Kings
Bible Class for Youth and Adults: Beginner's Guide: Introduction

**Notes in the New Testament**
Analyzing Notes in the Book of Matthew: Fulfillments of Old Testament Prophecies
Analyzing Notes in the Book of Mark: Finding Peace in Difficult Times
Analyzing Notes in the Book of Luke: The Divine Love of Jesus Revealed
Analyzing Notes in the Book of John: John's Contribution to the New Testament Scriptures
Analyzing Notes in the Book of the Acts of the Apostles: A Journey of Continuation in the Work of Jesus

**Overflying The Bible**
Symbols in the Bible: Healthy Christian Doctrine
Bible Introduction: Overflying The Bible from Genesis by Brethren in the Faith
Chronological Prophecy: Things That Will Happen on Earth
Bible Study: Genesis 1. Creation in Six Days

**PROPHETIC PROFILE**
Prophetic Profile: The Last Week, The Great Tribulation

## STUDY FROM SCRATCH
Bible Class for Youth and Adults: Beginner's Guide: The Pentateuch


### Teaching in the Bible class
Sunday School Lessons: 182 Bible Stories
Bible Class for Beginners: 50 Beautiful Lessons
Lessons for Sunday School: 62 Biblical Characters
How to Teach in Sunday School: A Guide for Bible Class Teachers


### Teaching in the Bible Classroom
Studying Teaching in the Bible Classroom: A Teacher's Guide


### The Education of Labor in the Bible
Analyzing the Education of Labor in Genesis: The Purpose of Life on Earth
Analyzing the Teaching of Labor in Exodus: From Slavery to Liberation
Analyzing the Labor Education in Leviticus: The Spirit of the Law at Work
Analyzing the Labor Education in Numbers: Israel's Desert Experience for Today's Challenges
Analyzing the Labor Education in Deuteronomy: A Perspective on Working Life Today
Analyzing Labor Education in Joshua and Judges: Motivation for Hard work!

Analyzing Labor Education in Ruth: A Reference for Self-growth and Self-improvement
Analyzing Labor Education in Samuel, kings and Chronicles: A Study of Leadership in Antiquity
Analyzing Labor Education in Ezra, Nehemiah, Esther: A Look at the Past to Orient our Future Work
Analyzing Labor Education in Job: Spiritual and Professional Example for Working Life
Analyzing Labor Education in Psalms: Ethics, Works and Words
Analyzing Labor Education in Proverbs
Analyzing Labor Education in Ecclesiastes: "Hard Work Under the Sun," The Lessons of Ecclesiastes
Analyzing Labor Education in Song of Solomon
Analyzing Labor Education in the Prophetic Books of Isaiah
Analyzing Labor Education in the Prophetic Books of Jeremiah and Lamentations
Analyzing Labor Education in the Prophetic Books of Ezekiel
Analyzing Labor Education in the Prophetic Books of Daniel
Analyzing Labor Education in the Prophetic Books of Hosea, Amos, Obadiah, Joel and Micah
Analyzing Labor Education in the Prophetic Books of Nahum, Habakkuk and Zephaniah
Analyzing Labor Education in the Prophetic Books of Haggai, Zechariah and Malachi
Analyzing Labor Education in Matthew's Gospel
Analyzing the Teaching of Work in Mark's Gospel
Analyzing Labor Education in Luke's Gospel
Analyzing Labor Education in John's Gospel
Analyzing Labor Education in the Acts of the Apostles
Analyzing Labor Education in the Epistle to the Romans
Analyzing Labor Education in the Epistle to the Corinthians
Analyzing Labor Education in the Epistles of Galatians, Ephesians and Philippians

Analyzing Labor Education in the Epistles to Colossians, Philemon and Thessalonians
Analyzing Labor Education in the Pastoral Letters: Timothy and Titus
Analyzing Labor Education in the General Letters and the Apocalypse
Analyzing Labor Education in the Four Gospels and the Acts
Analyzing Labor Education in the Epistles of the Apostle Paul
Analyzing Labor Education in the New Testament of the Bible
Analyzing Labor Education in Pentateuch
Analyzing Labor Education in the Historical Books: Applying the Bible to Practical Labor
Analyzing Labor Education in the Pentateuch and Books Historical
God's Guide for Work: Discovering God's Will for a Particular Job
Analyzing Labor Education in Poetic Books
Analyzing Labor Education in the Prophetic Books of the Bible
Analyzing Labor Education in the 12 Prophets of the Bible
Analyzing Labor Education in the Old Testament

## Standalone

Analyzing Notes in the 4 Gospels: Commentary Biblical
Analyzing What is to Come: God's Prophecies
The Prophetic Book Abdias: The Destruction of Edom
Bible Class for Youth and Adults: Beginner's Guide: I Don't Let Myself be Weetened

## About the Author

This bible study series is perfect for Christians of any level, from children to youth to adults. It provides an engaging and interactive way to learn the Bible, with activities and discussion topics that will help deepen your understanding of scripture and strengthen your faith. Whether you're a beginner or an experienced Christian, this series will help you grow in your knowledge of the Bible and strengthen your relationship with God. Led by brothers with exemplary testimonies and extensive knowledge of scripture, who congregate in the name of the Lord Jesus Christ throughout the world.